SHATTERED VESSELS

God's Way of Dealing with an Adulterous Husband

SHATTERED VESSELS: God's Way of Dealing with an Adulterous Husband

Copyright © 2014

Author Tiffany Buckner-Kameni

Email: info@anointedfire.com

All scriptures noted in this book were taken from the King James Bible unless otherwise noted.

ALL RIGHTS RESERVED. This book contains material protected under International and Federal Copyright Laws and Treaties. Any unauthorized reprint or use of this material is prohibited. No part of this book may be reproduced or transmitted in any form or by any means, electronic or mechanical, including photocopying, recording, or by any information storage and retrieval system, without express written permission from the author/publisher.

You may *not* sell or redistribute this book!

ISBN-13: 978-0692358351

ISBN-10: 0692358358

Disclaimer: I have tried to recreate events, locales and conversations from my memories of them. In order to maintain their anonymity in some instances I have changed the names of individuals and places, I may have changed some identifying characteristics and details such as physical properties, occupations and places of residence.

Although the author and publisher have made every effort to ensure that the information in this book was correct at press time, the author and publisher do not assume and hereby disclaim any liability to any party for any loss, damage, or disruption caused by errors or omissions, whether such errors or omissions result from negligence, accident, or any other cause.

Book Profile

In this book, I am going to go in depth to share with you what adultery is, what adultery does, and expose the spirits behind adultery. But first and foremost, I want to share the book's setup.

Bear with me as I share my testimony with you, and midways through the book, I will take you through one power-filled teaching after the other. I wanted to share my story with you first because I know the lies and games the enemy loves to play with women. I want you to see the Goliaths I've wrestled with so you won't think your Goliath is too big for you or that your giant is bigger than the giants that have harassed other women. The reason is, when we get into that kind of thinking, we'll often believe what we are wrestling with is too big or too strong for us, but when we know others have gone through, survived, and lived to be happy another day, we'll start to see our problems for what they are: temporary. When a woman is the victim of adultery, the enemy often fills her with lies about her situation. His goal is to:

1. Cause her to believe her situation is different and no one has ever been where she's currently at.
2. Cause her to believe her situation is going to consume her alive and she won't survive what she's going through.
3. Cause her to believe she's stupid for staying with a man who's mistreating her.
4. Cause her to question her own sanity as well as her choices.
5. Cause her to question the voice of GOD.
6. Cause her to believe GOD is mad at her, and her situation is being brought on by HIM.
7. Cause her to become upset with GOD so she won't turn to HIM in her hour of need.

Of course, there are many war tactics the enemy uses when trying to bring down a marriage and the people involved in that marriage. I wanted to share my story so you will see that your story is not uncommon. You're not stupid, you're not unattractive, and GOD is not mad at you. More than likely, you're just a woman who married the wrong man. If he is the one GOD sent to you,

you're just a woman who's experiencing the fall of the right man. It can happen, and sadly enough, many women have gone through what you're going through.

If you want to skip my testimony and go straight to the advice, you'll find the advice starts halfway through Chapter 6 (The Shame). I recommend you read the entire book, but if you need helpful tips right away, you can go straight to Chapter 6 or 7 and start reading from there.

Table of Contents

Book Profile..V
Introduction...XI
  Shattered Vessels...1
  Let's Talk About It...7
  The Experience...11
  The Lesson...33
  Hard Head, Soft Behind..................................41
  The Revelation..71
  The Shame...81
  The Reason He Cheated................................89
  Is He Cheating?...99
  Emotional Versus Physical Adultery..........113
  What Adultery Does to Women.................127
  The Truth about the Mistress......................139
  Living with a Cheating Man........................159
  Should You Leave or Stay?.........................169
  When You're Not Ready to Leave.............175
  In the Meantime..185
  To the Loved Ones of the Victim...............193
  To the Husband of the Victim 203
  Transitioning into Your New Reality..........221
  The Right Response to Adultery................237
  Common Scriptural Misinterpretations.245
  Surviving an Affair Together......................263
  How GOD Deals with an Adulterous
  Husband..289
  Effective Warfare Tactics............................309

Introduction

It's the middle of the night and you're awake. You look at the clock and feel the pain bearing down on your belly. Your husband isn't at home...*again*. You know what he's doing, and you probably know who he's doing it with, but the question is: When does it stop and how does it end? More than that, why hasn't GOD intervened? The truth is: Adultery has so many layers that go beyond our natural comprehension. Adultery isn't just an act we commit against our spouses; instead, the sin itself it rooted in idolatry.

There are a lot of books on the market that help women overcome their husbands' *past* affairs, but there aren't many that help women to survive their husbands' *current* affairs. After all, we need the truth more when we're in the midst of a trial than we do when we've come out of that trial.

In Shattered Vessels: God's Way of Dealing With an Adulterous Husband, Author Tiffany Buckner-Kameni will pick apart the spirits behind adultery and help you to understand your rights as a wife. If you're enduring an adulterous husband, the best thing to do is educate yourself about your rights with GOD. Additionally, you need to get a better understanding of what you can expect from GOD. You are not on this journey alone. Many women have gone before you; some have fallen along the way, while others have passed their tests to come out with testimonies. Getting the understanding you'll need will not only make the journey easier, but it will help you to see what's ahead of you as opposed to focusing on what you're going through.

Shattered Vessels

Beautiful and angelic, she lifts her weeping eyes to the heavens. Her beauty has been challenged by the torments she's endured. Her heart is heavy with grief; so heavy, she can hear it beating from within her broken soul. Her heart has been used as a weapon against her, and the man wielding that weapon is the man she'd entrusted with it. He's a man who's vowed to love, protect, and honor her all the days of his life. *He lied.* Instead, he's doing the very opposite of what he's promised to do.

With every breath she breathes, she can feel the sorrow trying to consume her. Her peace has been stolen, and now, her mind is nothing less than a war zone where the enemy tortures her day-in and day-out. She looks to the man who she loves so dearly for help, but he's the one who's waged war against her. Instead of fighting with her, he's fighting against her. He's familiar

Shattered Vessels

and unrecognizable at the same time. She struggles to remember the good times, but the sounds of laughter that once played in her head are now drowned out by the sounds of an agonizing cry coming from within the depths of her soul. This piercing cry has deafened her to the sounds of her children and everyone else around her.

She is separated from the truth by her reality. She stands on the other side of the lies she's been told, trying to find some form of truth in the words she hear every day. Nevertheless, every lie she chooses crumbles in her hands.

The once fragile woman is now broken, shattered by the impact of every new revelation of her lover's dealings. Every wicked word and new revelation crushes her already broken heart. And now, she is nothing but a shell of the woman she once was. She's distracted by her reality and fearful of what's ahead. Like a lioness, she roars in anger against the force that's raging up against

Shattered Vessels

her heart, but who is she kidding? As fierce as she appears to be on the outside, she's nothing but a scared kitten on the inside. At the same time, her silent roars go unheard by many and are ignored by the man who's piercing her heart. He wants her to be silent, because her groanings serve as a painful reminder to him that his warped dreams will end in a nightmare. Her tears tell a story that he doesn't want to read; instead, he simply wants the confident woman who's expecting a monogamous relationship to pass away and make room for a competitive and lowly woman who'll do anything to keep him around. Nevertheless, she continues to fight with her words and beg with her eyes for her merciless lover to have mercy upon her broken soul. Who is she? She's the wife of an adulterer.

I can't tell you how many times I've spoken with heartbroken women, women who were grieving what they feared was the inevitable destruction of their marriages. Truthfully, hearing a heartbroken woman pouring her heart out never gets any easier. I want to tell her that GOD will chase the mistress away, swiftly punish her husband, and all will return to normal in their marriage within a matter of minutes, but I can't. That's because every marriage doesn't end the same way. Some marriages continue and the couples learn to put what's happened behind them. Other marriages have never recovered from adultery, and then, there are those marriages that did not end, but they'd changed so drastically that neither of the parties involved were happy. So, I take the time out to tell her my story. I share with her what I'd gone through in the two marriages I'd entered in my rebellious years. I listen carefully, making sure I don't step on her already fragile heart. All the same, as painful as it may be, I have to destroy the lies she's told herself or the lies her husband has told her. That's because <u>she can't be free until she accepts the truth</u>.

Adultery is a huge problem in the United States and abroad. Truthfully, it's an epidemic in today's society. That's because modern day couples are taught to be problem-focused as opposed to solution-oriented. Instead of trying to fix the mounting problems that's found in all marriages, some people opt to replace their spouses with people they think are better suited for themselves. Most people simply don't know how to be married, so they enter a GOD-instituted idea (marriage), but they bring conditions with them. When one spouse offends the other, it is not uncommon for the offended spouse to seek comfort in another man or woman's arms. Additionally, today's media has become the primary source of information with the average couple, replacing the Bible study and church they'll need to make their marriage work. Ironically enough, modern day media teaches people to think individually as opposed to operating as a unit. Such thinking leads a man astray. For a couple to make it, they must operate as a united front, and for this reason, Satan encourages division in a marriage. All too often, this division comes in the form of "the other woman".

Shattered Vessels

Regardless of what a woman endures, she's still a vessel that was created by GOD, but when adultery enters her life, she becomes a shattered vessel.

What exactly is a shattered vessel? We all know a vessel is a large boat, often used to carry cargo from one place to the other. As vessels of GOD, we are used by GOD to carry HIS WORD to the nations. When a woman has a broken heart, she begins to carry the pain within her, and she'll often share that pain with others. She is then a shattered vessel, a woman who has to be healed and restored by the very hand of the GOD who created her.

Let's Talk About It

Honestly, I am not comfortable sharing my life's experiences with people through books. I don't mind sharing them one-on-one with people, but I have had to be delivered from a cultural mindset that demands I keep "my business" quiet. I don't care about being labeled or misjudged by people; my concern is for the people involved in the stories I'm about to tell you. I've said it before, and I'll reiterate it here. I've forgiven the men from my past, but all too often, GOD calls me to share my testimonies with others so they can be saved, healed, and delivered. Nevertheless, speaking publicly about situations that involve others, people who've probably been delivered and are regretful of their past choices, can be somewhat bothersome to me. But if sharing my testimony helps you or someone else in any way, it is well worth me coming outside of my comfort zone.

In this book, I'm about to bear it all for you. I want

you to see how "stupid" I was. After all, that's what most women who are victims of adultery call themselves when they don't have the strength to leave their philandering husbands. I want you to know how low my self-perception was, because most women who are victims of adultery don't realize how much their husbands' adulteries have torn them down, leaving nothing but their faith, or lack thereof, on display. I want you to see that your situation is not unique; you are not "stupid", and you can be healed and delivered from an adulterous spouse...*if that's what you want.* For the sake of restoring you and any other woman who desires to be restored, I am going to bear my soul and my experiences in this book, and it's not going to be pretty. You <u>will</u> shake your head at my choices. You may even become upset with me, and that's okay. My goal isn't to get fans, but to show you that as bad as your situation may seem, someone's been through far worse, and someone's been even stupider than you think you're being. You will come to understand that there is life after an adulterous affair. You just

Let's Talk About It

have to embrace it to live it. All the same, I'm going to share with you what GOD has taught me along the way.

If you don't know, I've been married twice, and in both marriages, I was the victim of adultery. In an attempt to "get revenge", I'd even committed adultery against one of the husbands I'd chosen for myself. I encourage you to read this book in its entirety so you can learn the lessons I had to learn without enduring the experiences I had to endure. Healing is available for you, and the answers you seek can be found within the pages of your heart, but I pray this book will help you to turn those pages until you figure out what decision is best for you.

I will coach, comfort, and love on you along the way, but I won't tell you any lies, even if lies are what you want.

Last, but not least, every now and again, I come across a man who's offended that my articles and

Let's Talk About It

books are oftentimes tailored for women and not men. I've never been a man *(I am perfectly happy being a woman)*, so I only speak to men when GOD gives me the green-light to do so, but at this time, HE keeps instructing me to address the women. So, if you happen to be a guy, please know that the information in this book can be beneficial to you as well, but I won't step into an arena until I've been invited (by GOD) to enter that arena. With that being said, please don't take offense with me speaking to the sisters about adulterous men. I am fully aware that there are plenty of adulterous women out there; after all, I've lost two uncles (death by violence) because of their adulterous wives. Maybe someday, GOD will have me to write a book or an article to address men about adulterous women, but as of right now, I'm called to minister to the women of GOD about their relationships.

The Experience

I raised my head to look at the clock. It was three o'clock in the morning and Taylor (the man I was married to) still hadn't come home. He'd stormed out the night before after purposely starting an argument. This had become the norm in our home. Every Friday evening, we'd get into a heated fight about some of the silliest things, and he'd storm out the house. Normally, he'd return home in the middle of the night, but he was becoming more and more brazen. He'd gone from staying out until two or three in the morning to coming home after daybreak, and I was weary with grief.

I looked around the room I was in. I was sitting on the couch in our den, watching the new big screen television set I'd just bought for him. As I reviewed the room, I started inwardly coaching myself. I told myself how good of a woman I was, and I told myself I would survive what I was going through.

The Experience

But I didn't know how. After all, adultery felt very much like a slow and agonizing death. All I could think of was how happy he was making someone else at my expense. The pain was intense. Truthfully, I don't think "intense" fairly describes what it's like to sit at home, knowing your husband is out there having sex with someone else. Sure, like most men, he denied his affairs, but like most women, I knew better. I knew him and I'd always known when he was having an affair.

Every time Taylor would pull the "argue and leave" stunt, I would go out looking for him. I wanted to catch him in the act because, for some silly reason, I thought catching him would cause him to finally humble himself and talk to me. I was willing to endure a divorce; after all, the pain I was living in had become almost unbearable. But I didn't want to walk away with my suspicions. I wanted concrete evidence that Taylor was having an affair, even though I had enough evidence to have him convicted in every court in America five times over. Honestly, now that I'm no longer in that marriage

The Experience

(or that pain), I can fairly assess my intentions. I'd given up on Taylor, but I didn't know how to be without the man I'd come to love more than I loved myself. A divorce meant starting over and dividing up our assets, and for me, a divorce meant moving back into my mother's house. My siblings were still at my mother's house and we'd had rather contentious relationships with one another, so I cringed at the idea of having to return to my mother's house. I was confused and I was taking life and the impact of what I was going through one breath at a time.

Nevertheless, that particular night was different than the nights before. I hadn't gone out searching for my elusive husband. Instead, I could feel the presence of GOD with me. I knew HE was there, and I felt HE was finally answering my prayers and visiting my pain. I needed the pain to stop because, like most women, I wanted my husband to experience just how painful his adulterous affairs were. I'd told him using as many words as I'd known, but I was reaching the

The Experience

point where I was looking at other ways of hurting him that didn't involve words. *I felt like I was losing my mind.* Needless to say, I loved the LORD, but I hadn't completely underwent the renewing of my mind. I had been very prayerful, crying many nights and begging GOD to visit my pain and help me, but when I didn't hear back from Heaven, I raised hell in my house. I was definitely double-minded and unstable in all my ways.

That night, a sudden calm came over me and I knew everything was going to be alright. For the first time, I'd made peace with the idea of letting go. I'd resolved myself to the understanding that I'd done all I could do, and my marriage would end in divorce. I let the tears fall as I drifted peacefully to sleep.

While asleep, I began to dream. In the dream, I was standing in the living room of our house and there were two men in the house. One of the men was an uncle of mine who worked with Taylor, and the other man was clearly a man of authority,

The Experience

possibly his boss. Both men were looking into the den and I was curious to see what they were looking at. After all, my uncle was shaking his head in disappointment at whatever it was he was seeing, and the other man was writing a report. Both men were in their work uniforms.

I walked over to the doorway and stood between them, looking up at my uncle as he continued to shake his head in disappointment. I turned my head to see what he was looking at, and there was a bed in my den. In the bed, I saw Taylor and his mistress having sex. Truthfully, I'd never seen that particular mistress before. I'd seen a couple before her, but not her. In the dream, I could see her eyeglasses on the nightstand, and they (Taylor and his mistress) were so lost in the passion, they hadn't noticed the three of us standing in the doorway. Suddenly, I looked up at my uncle and said, "She's pregnant now. There's no way she's not pregnant." After those words, I woke up.

When I opened my eyes, I immediately began to

The Experience

weep. GOD had finally answered my prayer that HE reveal to me the truth about what was going on with Taylor. I was in a lot of pain, but with that pain came a sense of relief. The truth was finally out, and even though I believed Taylor would continue to lie about his indiscretions, I knew I'd heard from GOD, and HE cannot tell a lie.

Suddenly, I heard a car pulling into the driveway. I knew it was Taylor, so I began to wipe the tears away from my eyes. After all, I knew if he saw me crying, he'd get upset and leave again, and I didn't want that. I needed to talk with him and let him know I was okay with us breaking up. My heart raced as I listened to the sound of the living room door being unlocked. I'd slept on the couch in the den and could see Taylor's head as he came through the door. *My stomach was in knots.* I was tired of arguing and I was tired of being depressed. I just wanted the relationship to be over with; plus, according to the dream, his mistress was pregnant, and I knew I wasn't going to stick around if that were true. I felt like a

The Experience

tortured prisoner begging for my torturer to put me out of my misery.

Taylor came into the house and entered the den. For some reason, he looked humbled...not like the angry man who'd dressed up, started a fight, and stormed out the night before. "I need to talk to you," I said softly. "I don't want to fight anymore. Please just sit down and let me talk to you." To my surprise, he sat down and I told him I wanted a divorce. I was gentle with my words because I didn't want to set off another argument. I told him he could take whatever he wanted, but I was moving back home with my mother. Surprisingly enough, he remained silent as I spoke. I studied his face and was shocked that I didn't see any signs of anger. I just wanted the pain to stop and divorce appeared more merciful than enduring another day of Taylor's antics. As I was speaking with him, I began to reveal my dream to him. I described his mistress in full detail and told him she was pregnant. At that moment, he got off the couch and lowered himself to his knees. He made

The Experience

his way toward me (we were on a sectional couch) on his knees and he began to apologize for everything he'd done. Without warning, he began to confess his affairs with other women. He appeared to be hurting on the inside as he confirmed my worst nightmare and suspicions. Even though the truth hurt, I felt relieved. *I wasn't crazy after all.* Truthfully, I think that knowing I wasn't losing my mind was one of the greatest rewards in it all because there were many days I'd weighed what he was saying against what I felt in my heart, and I had started to believe that something was wrong with me. *A sound mind is one of the casualties suffered in adultery.*

"Is she pregnant?" I asked. He stopped and stared at me, and I could see the fear in his eyes. Taylor stared at me for what felt like forever before answering. "I don't know," he responded. "But I think she is because she's been acting really strange lately." I tried to contain the pain that was growing within my belly. I needed to remain calm; after all, Taylor was finally talking and I didn't want

The Experience

to upset him. "Call her," I said. "Ask her if she's pregnant." By this time, he'd already called one of his mistresses and told her that he would no longer see her because he "wanted to work things out with his wife." He told her not to call him anymore, and he made sure I could hear her speaking so I'd know he was actually talking to her. When he called the second mistress (the one I'd dreamed of), he initially couldn't reach her, so he left a message on her answering machine. I could tell he didn't want to address her personally, so he'd called her home knowing that she was at work. But I wanted to know if she was pregnant, so I urged him to call her at work, and he finally obliged.

I could hear her voice as she yelled at him. She'd called home just moments earlier and listened to his message on her answering machine. He kept asking her if she was pregnant, and at first, she kept asking him his reason for wanting to know. Finally, her words shattered my heart in the worst way. "Yes, I'm pregnant, but I wasn't going to tell

The Experience

you because I knew you wouldn't leave your wife!" He looked over at me and shook his head in affirmation. At that moment, I felt like I couldn't breathe. I lost all of my strength and I just let myself drop to the floor. I was fully conscious, but the pain was just too great. After all, I'd just suffered my second miscarriage, and here it was that the man I loved so dearly had cheated on me and gotten someone else pregnant. He hung up the phone and tried to help me get off the floor, but I didn't want to get up. I just wanted to lay there and cry. *I needed to lie there and cry.*

Moments later, I found myself on the couch being caressed by the man who'd just ripped my soul in half. "I don't think it's my baby," he said. "She has a boyfriend, too." I couldn't speak. Like any red-blooded wife, I wanted his words to be true, but at the same time, I knew my worst nightmare had just come true. My marriage was over to me, but Taylor was determined to right his wrongs. He reasoned with me to stay with him, promising to be a better man, never cheat on me again, and to

The Experience

get me into the house we'd been trying to buy. *He began to dangle my dreams in front of me.* My dream was that we got into the house we'd just applied for, have children, and live happily (and successfully) ever after. Nevertheless, the news of Taylor's mistress and their growing family placed two options in my path. I could go back to my mother's house and go through the grieving process; all the while, fighting with my siblings, or I could take a chance with the man I loved so much and possibly have the life I'd dreamed of having with him if I could only get over the hurdle that was in front of me. I decided to push forward with him. I reasoned from within that he'd finally come around to confessing and he'd ended his affairs with his mistresses. Now, all we had to do was heal.

Healing proved to be a lot harder than I'd anticipated. Now that I knew the adultery had occurred, I couldn't get rid of the thoughts of Taylor having sex with other women. Those imaginations haunted me day-in and day-out. I

The Experience

asked him many questions, I cried a lot, and I attempted to rebuild my self-worth through his answers. It goes without saying, however, that with no professional counseling, neither he nor I knew how to heal without hurting one another. I believed he should let me ask as many questions as I needed to ask so I could heal. He believed we needed to put the past behind us and stop talking about what happened. Needless to say, the fights started flaring up again and it wasn't long before Taylor was back to being Taylor.

The final straw came one day when I'd returned home from work and pressed redial on our home phone. Taylor had the phone sitting next to him, and I knew he wasn't the type of man who liked to speak on the phone; plus, he rarely used the home phone, so I snatched the phone and hit redial. My agony intensified as I watched his mistress's number pop up on the screen. I immediately hung up the phone and threw it back next to him. "I was only returning her call," he explained.

The Experience

At that time, we were trying to buy a house, and I'd run into an ex-boyfriend of mine while in the process of collecting the paperwork we needed to get that house. *Of course, Satan was setting me up.* The ex was an older guy, a man I'd dated when I was young and unsaved. I wasn't physically attracted to him, but he was a very successful man, so my initial relationship with him was all about advancing myself, and his initial relationship with me was all about having a young woman to show off. We hadn't exchanged numbers when I'd seen him again, but he'd told me where his company was located and he'd bragged about how much money his company had made the year prior. By this time, I was much more mature than I had been when I'd dated him years prior, so the money didn't impress me....*much*. I was starved of affection and just wanted to feel loved again. Plus, I'd always loved how he looked at me. He made me feel beautiful, wanted, and like I deserved the best of what life had to offer.

The Experience

After I'd pressed redial and discovered Taylor was back to his old ways, I stood in the doorway of the den staring at him. After all of the promises he'd made to me, he'd returned to his philandering ways almost immediately. I stormed into my bedroom and began to pick out something to wear. I'd made up my mind. I was going to go and give my body to my ex, and then, Taylor would know how it felt to deal with adultery. My thoughts were all over the place. I began to ignore the voice of GOD because I was still young in the faith and I was in full submission to my emotions. I felt betrayed once again, and I was determined to exact my revenge.

I turned on the water in the bathtub and let my dark thoughts take over. In a way, I wanted Taylor to come and stop me from doing what I was about to do, but I knew he would purposely avoid me so he wouldn't have to talk about what he'd done. Nevertheless, as foolish as it may be, I held out hope that he would stop me before I got out that door. After all, I wasn't an adulteress...or at least,

The Experience

that's what I told myself. I was a woman in a lot of pain looking for a way to make that pain stop.

After I'd dressed and put on some makeup, I grabbed my purse and headed toward the front door. I stopped and looked over at Taylor as he was sitting in the den. I wanted him to see how beautiful I was. I wanted him to question where I was going and why I was looking so good. "I'm going to the mall," I said with a smile on my face. "Do you want to come with me?" I already knew what his answer was going to be. After all, he'd stopped going places with me after he'd started his latest affair, using every home alone opportunity he had to call his mistresses. "No? Okay. I'll be back in a couple of hours," I said. I kept staring at him, but he wouldn't look at me. I wanted him to see me, but he'd intentionally fixated his eyes on the television in front of him. I smiled on the outside, but on the inside, I was an unquenchable inferno. I walked out the front door, got into my car, and drove to my ex's office. It was now late and dark outside, but I knew he'd be in

The Experience

the office, likely wrapping things up to go home. I knew he was still interested in me because of the looks he'd given me the few times I'd run into him. At the same time, his office wasn't too far from my house. I parked my car on the other side of his office, walked through the door and saw that he was on the phone. *I didn't care.* I wanted revenge, so I started undressing him before he could even address me. Needless to say, he was shocked but willing. And from there, the affair began.

After leaving his office, I was expecting to feel some sort of satisfaction in knowing that I'd just done to Taylor what he'd been doing to me for years. I'd just given "his" body away. Nevertheless, I didn't feel that sense of vindication I so longed for. Instead, I felt dirty. For more than five years, I'd prided myself on being a faithful wife, and in the blink of a blind eye, my virtue was over. The worst of it all was that I'd just sinned against GOD while trying to get revenge against Taylor. I felt sick to my stomach and the guilt

The Experience

made it far worse. I didn't like the way I felt. My thoughts went to Taylor and his two-timing ways. How could he shut off his feelings and lie down with someone else? Of course, the answer was clear: He wasn't saved. He was a man of the world, but I was a woman of GOD, or better yet, a babe in CHRIST. I felt too ashamed to even try to talk to GOD. But to offset those feelings were feelings of being wanted by a man. You see, Taylor had started making me feel undesired, unwanted, and just plain ugly, but the ever-so-willing ex of mine made me feel beautiful, desired, and needed. I was able to lift my head again and not be distracted by every woman who looked like Taylor's type. So, for one month, I engaged in an adulterous affair with my ex. For one month, I felt as if I was separated from GOD, but I kept begging for HIS forgiveness, and one day, I found myself begging for something entirely different from GOD. I started pleading with HIM to make me stop the affair because I felt like I didn't know how to stop on my own. Again, I wasn't attracted to the ex, nor was I enjoying sex with him, but I'd

The Experience

become addicted to feeling wanted and needed. I'd realized my whole reason for being with him had shifted from revenge to an all-too-consuming need to feel wanted and loved, if but for just fifteen minutes. At home, I was feeling starved of affection. There were no hugs or any "I love yous" anymore, and I couldn't enjoy the sex because I kept imagining him doing to his mistresses what he was doing to me. We were living and behaving like roommates with benefits.

GOD answered my prayers and put a stop to that affair a month after it had begun. One day, I'd gone to the ex's house, but for the first time, I prayed while on my way there, instead of begging for forgiveness after I left. I was honest with GOD. I told HIM I couldn't stop on my own; I needed HIM to stop me. I didn't want to hurt the LORD anymore. I asked HIM to intervene and take the desires away.
When I arrived at the ex's house, everything went its usual pace. We sat on the couch talking for a short time, pretending to be interested in one

The Experience

another's conversations, and then, I'd looked at the clock and realized we'd better do what I'd come to do so I could go home.

The sex that day was worse than awful, and at the same time, I didn't feel the boost of confidence I'd come there to get. GOD delivered me by making me feel loved and wanted by HIM, so when I tried to feel those things with that man, I ended up feeling deprived of them instead. Instead of him adding to me, I felt as if he was taking away from me. The sex felt empty and I wanted it to be over quickly, but instead, it seemed like the longest and most frustrating encounter I'd ever had with him.

When I got into my car to leave, instead of feeling those overwhelming feelings of guilt and dread, I felt joyful. Tears rolled down my face as I truly repented to GOD for what I'd done, and I declared to HIM that I'd never do it again. I thanked HIM for delivering me as I drove to my house. At that moment, GOD began to explain to me that HE'D

The Experience

heard me all those times I'd asked HIM to show me the truth about Taylor, but HE hadn't shown me because I wasn't ready. HE knew I would sin against HIM and against my husband. HE knew I wasn't spiritually mature enough to know the truth, so he was protecting me instead of ignoring me. When HE'D given me the dream, HE'D done so because I'd asked for that revelation, and at the same time, HE wanted to show me what was on the inside of me. I needed to be delivered from so many things, adultery being one of them, and unforgiveness being another. Of course, I felt grieved. GOD had been holding, protecting, and guiding me all along, and I couldn't see past getting back at the man GOD had been protecting me from. I repented that day, and immediately, my mind was renewed. I knew I'd never engage in adultery again, but I also knew my marriage was definitely over. After all, I'd lost my virtuous crown and I didn't feel worthy of being married, even though the man I was married to had tarnished me many times.

The Experience

Taylor and I were finally approved for the home we wanted. We got into the house we'd applied for, and we stayed there for a year before I learned he had rekindled his relationship with the woman who'd had his child. Once again, he started instigating fights every Friday evening, and I recognized that pattern immediately. He then started sleeping out of the house, blaming me for his decision to sleep over at a *friend's* house. Of course, he said the friend was a male and that I didn't know him. I questioned how he was getting to work, and he said that his mysterious friend had been taking him. I knew better, so I staked out his job one morning and saw his mistress dropping him off. Not long after that, I filed for divorce. I'd realized that he was not only living with his mistress, but his decision to do so verified that the child was indeed his child and he was playing the family man with them; all the while, attempting to make me feel as if his decision to stay "at a friend's house" was my fault.

After we started the divorce proceedings, I

The Experience

honestly felt relieved. I was hurt, but the pain I felt didn't hold a candle to the pain I'd endured while with him. The pain I was enduring felt far more merciful, and, of course, I'd come to understand that GOD was carrying me through it all. To be free of him and any feelings of betrayal, hatred, or confusion, I asked GOD to put forgiveness in me for Taylor and his mistresses and GOD did. Nevertheless, there were still many more lessons to be learned.

The Lesson

There was a lot to be learned from Taylor's affairs and my own affair, and I was eager to get the knowledge I needed to finally find my place in peace once again. At that time, I took a portion of the lesson, but I didn't let GOD complete what HE wanted to do in me. I was still battling with generational thinking, fears that had been intensified by my broken relationship with Taylor, and a biological clock that seemed to be going off in my head. I wanted to be married and I wanted to have children, but I didn't want to endure the changes GOD was making in me to prep me for the life HE'D prepared for me.

Here are a few lessons I learned:
1. There is clearly a reason GOD allows us to divorce a spouse once that spouse has committed adultery. That reason is: divorce feels a lot like dealing with the death of a loved one, but adultery feels a lot like

The Lesson

watching a loved one repeatedly die a slow and agonizing death while you stand there helpless. Adultery is merciless, but GOD is merciful. Sometimes, the only way to "put us out of our misery" is to separate us from the source of our pain.

2. GOD hates a divorce, but HE also hates adultery. Idolatry is spiritual adultery, and idolatry is when a person worships another god, and, of course, the proper name for another god is an idol. When a nation committed idolatry against GOD, it hurt HIM so much that HE has been known to pour out HIS wrath upon that nation, but, of course, HE held some of HIS wrath back. The full wrath of GOD is without mercy. Hell is GOD'S wrath unrestrained; meaning, there is no mercy or love there. Adultery, to us, is almost as painful as idolatry is to GOD, and that's why the spouse who's being victimized oftentimes becomes wrathful, and in many cases, dangerous. Any time adultery is in a marriage, jealousy

The Lesson

will be in that marriage, and the spirit of jealousy has been known to lead people down some pretty dark paths.

3. Sometimes, GOD doesn't give us the answers we so crave because HE knows we can't handle those answers. HE will never place more on us than we can bear. Nevertheless, if we pursue those answers, GOD will turn on the lights for us so we can see what's really going on. From there, whatever sin is still within us will rise to the top and began to stake its claim on our souls. In other words, GOD will oftentimes protect us from ourselves by keeping us from seeing what our spouses are doing until we're spiritually mature enough to handle the truth.

4. A man is the head of his home, and therefore, can cause the body (family) to stumble. For this reason, a woman should always let GOD choose her husband for her because the wrong man will lead her in the wrong direction, and even though she

The Lesson

may resist his ways, she will likely eventually succumb to his thinking patterns.

5. We shouldn't marry until we've been fully delivered from wrongful thinking. Wrongful thinking leads us into idolatry, adultery, revengeful mentalities, thoughts of suicide, and thoughts of murder. Always remember that the spirit is willing, but the flesh is weak.

6. An adulterous spouse will continue to cheat, regardless of how his spouse feels about his affairs. No amount of tears, arguments, or words will convince such a soul to turn away from his adulteries; therefore, the spouse on the receiving end has a choice: stay and accept what the other spouse is doing or leave. All too often, women decide to stay and fight, and this almost always ends badly. If you're going to stay, don't fight, and if you're going to fight, don't stay.

7. If your spouse is having an affair, it's not your fault. Before I'd discovered Taylor's

The Lesson

adulteries, I'd done everything underneath the sun to make him happy. I was so confident in my marriage, I'd even tried rebuking a friend whose husband had been cheating on her. I'd rebuked her for not sleeping with her husband any time he wanted sex. I will never forget her words. She said, "Tiffany, I don't care how much sex you have with a man. You can spin around on him while holding onto a ceiling fan, but if he's a cheater, he's going to cheat on you anyway." I was so disappointed in her because I felt she was being naïve. Once I discovered Taylor was indeed having an affair, I froze in dismay, staring at the wall for what felt like hours.

8. When you love and fear the LORD, you open yourself up to hear from HIM. When your spouse is cheating, HIS voice will warn you from the inside, but all too often, we think we're going crazy when GOD'S words don't match up with our lovers' words. So, in many cases, women stay

The Lesson

with their adulterous husbands; all the while, going through their cellphones, following them around town, and conducting all types of silly investigations trying to catch their husbands in their own lies. When GOD speaks to you, you don't need any more evidence, you simply need to make up your mind as to what you want to do about what GOD has revealed.

9. When a wife is suffering because of her husband's adulteries, in many cases, she can't trust her own thoughts...especially when those thoughts are dark. That same devil that encouraged her husband to engage in an affair is the very devil that will whisper in her ears and tell her how to catch him. When I endured adultery for the first time, I considered many things, including harming the man I was married to. That's because, at that time, my relationship with Taylor was idolatrous. I'd unknowingly placed him before GOD, and this was evidenced in my decision to sin

The Lesson

against GOD for the sake of getting revenge against him.

10. A wife should never look for evidence she's not ready to accept. In most cases, when a man cheats, his wife will lose her peace, and because this peace is vital to her everyday living, she will seek to retrieve her peace by conducting all kinds of maddening investigations. What she doesn't realize, however, is that she isn't ready just yet for the truth. When she does find the truth, all of her emotions hit her at once, and there have been cases where women have taken the lives of their husbands, their husbands' mistresses, or their own lives. If you're not ready for the truth, be still and know that GOD has appointed the right time to reveal the truth to you. When you're ready for the truth, the truth will come to you.

Of course, there were, and are, many more lessons, but the point is, you can't change a man, nor should you sin against GOD or yourself trying

The Lesson

to teach him a lesson. Vengeance belongs to GOD, but any time you deal with an adulterous spouse, you will be tempted to take revenge, whether that revenge be through having an adulterous affair of your own or hurting your spouse. I survived that marriage and all that it entailed, and I grew wiser from it.

Hard Head, Soft Behind

I remember the older folks used to say, "A hard head makes a soft behind." I'd been that hard-headed girl on the wrong side of a swinging belt, so I understood that cliché very well. I'd been that hard-headed girl who'd endured a lot of hurt because of the choices I'd made. After my marriage to Taylor ended, and we started divorce proceedings, you would've thought I'd learned my lesson and I'd learned it well, but I didn't. I knew I loved GOD and I knew I was a good woman. I'd blamed the ending of the first marriage entirely on Taylor, so I thought I was the perfect candidate for marriage. In my mind, I was a good woman, and if I met a good man, we'd have a great marriage.

I was still going through a divorce from Taylor when I'd met the man who'd be my second husband. Roger was an African man from Cameroon, and I believed with every fiber of my warped understanding that he would make a great

husband. I was still obviously battling some strongholds and didn't want to understand that I wasn't ready to be anyone's wife, nor should I be entertaining another man while still married. I reasoned within myself that I was going through a divorce and would be single very soon, so it had to be okay for me to date the new guy.
I was wrong.

I was anxious to receive those final divorce papers so I could marry my illegal fiancé. He was going to school in Europe, and even though I was fully against Internet relationships, I'd decided to give him a chance. After all, I was not on any dating websites, nor had I met him intentionally. He'd simply reached out to me because I was advertising a website I had at that time, and he wanted to be a part of that website. My curiosity got the best of me, so I responded to his chats every time he sent them. I wanted to know more about his country and his culture. Again, I was born a poor girl, so I hadn't experienced a whole lot in my life. In the city I'd grown up in, there weren't a lot of foreigners. Truthfully, I can only remember a few Asians and Indians, but I don't think I'd ever met someone from Africa before meeting Roger. Speaking with someone from another country and learning about that person's culture was very fascinating to me. While speaking with him, I found myself liking him more and more. We'd exchanged numbers and he'd dispelled some of my biggest fears about foreign men. We flirted with each other, and finally surrendered to the idea of entering a relationship with one another. I had always been a huge risk-taker, so dating Roger was exciting to me. The whole concept of dating someone from another country who I'd met online wasn't a big surprise to the people who knew me. After all, I'd always prided myself in taking risks and pushing the limits of what's right and what's wrong. I was overjoyed about the connection, especially after Roger told me he didn't have any kids, he was Christian (Catholic, actually), and he didn't believe in divorce. He said that his parents had remained married for decades, all the way up until his father's death. I told him how my first marriage had ended and the things I'd gone through in that marriage, and he responded the way I wanted him to respond. He seemed to be against the whole idea of adultery, and he told me he would never cheat on me...*if I were his wife.* I didn't realize I needed to be healed, and, of course, divorced, before I entered a new relationship; therefore, my marriage to him was really based on what I felt I hadn't received from Taylor. His marriage to me, on the other hand, was questionable. I didn't want to entertain the idea that he was interested in me for the sake of getting a green card, even though my family and friends had warned me repeatedly. After all, he was already in the western world (Europe), and he was in school studying to be a bio-engineer. *What else could he possibly want from me?*

After my first marriage was terminated, Roger and I began to plan our wedding. We'd known each other for close to a year by then, we'd already met face-to-face, and we'd already established a soul

Hard Head, Soft Behind

tie with one another through our adulterous dealings. *My divorce hadn't been finalized before we'd "gotten together" so I was definitely guilty of the sin of adultery.* Even though I knew GOD wasn't pleased with how I'd went about doing things, I thought I could make it up to GOD after getting married. In other words, I tried to put me first and GOD second, and as you'll come to see, that did not work out in my favor.

We decided to get married in Denmark because it was easier and cheaper to marry there, and for me, it was the opportunity to go to another country. I'd been to Germany, and Roger had taken me to many other countries in Europe, so getting married in Denmark seemed like a bonus. I was in love, swept away by the euphoria often found in new relationships, and floating on the lies Roger told me and the lies I'd told myself. After we'd married, we began to plan our lives together. Where would we live? Roger had said he wanted to live in Germany, but I insisted that we live in the United States. By that time, I was speaking with his sister, Mara, every day. His sister lived in Atlanta and told me to encourage him to come to the States because school and life would be easier for us here. Of course, he gave in pretty easily and we decided to live in the States for a while. He said he wanted to eventually move back to Europe, and from there, back to Cameroon. I agreed with his plans initially, hoping I could change his mind.

It didn't take long for me to realize I'd made a huge mistake. Roger was now my husband, and after a few applications and application fees, I was able to get him clearance to begin his life in the United States. His first stop was to his sister's house, and we'd agreed that I'd go to Georgia so we could be together. At the same time, he'd just been accepted into a program in Germany that would allow him to write his thesis, and the company was going to pay for his housing and food, so we'd decided to go back to Germany for six months until he finished his thesis. Nevertheless, in the meantime, we'd decided to

Hard Head, Soft Behind

enjoy a week or two of American living before heading to Europe.

I arrived at Mara's house a day before Roger's flight was set to land. I'd already met Mara before, and I was comfortable going to her house because we'd gotten along so well initially. I'd brought my little sister with me, and the two of us had taken a bus from Mississippi to Georgia.

Once I arrived at Mara's house, one of the first things I began to notice was how controlling she was. I'd noticed this the first time I'd met her, but I'd told myself she was really a nice person underneath it all. We'd had many "normal" conversations before, so I just brushed our first meeting off as her being stressed out. I was determined to be on her "good side" until I realized she didn't have one.

One of the first things I noticed when I walked into Mara's apartment was a young woman sitting in her living room, and I recognized her almost immediately. I'd initially seen her on a social network Roger and I were on. The young lady (Olivia) posted a lot of comments under Roger's photos and I'd been receiving notifications because I'd commented under those same photos. I'd noticed her comments were flirtatious; plus, she'd told Roger to call her, so I'd clicked on her profile and went to her photos to see who she was. I saw that she was also living in Atlanta, and Roger had been flirtatiously commenting under her photos as well. I immediately called and confronted him. He'd told me the mysterious woman was the daughter of his sister's best friend and that their communications were not only harmless, but they were normal for his culture. To test his theory, I sent her a friend request, and she immediately declined my request.

Fast forward back to Mara's living room.....I was sitting on the couch, staring at this young lady. I could tell that she was pretty young, maybe ten years younger than Roger and I. She was polite and I decided to not entertain the idea that she could possibly be my husband's girlfriend, or maybe even his wife.

The next day, Roger arrived in the States and we went to the airport to pick him up. I remember Mara being super agitated because he seemed to be taking too long getting his luggage. Again, I brushed it off as stress. I did wonder, however, why Olivia was tagging along with us. I noticed that she'd put an extra effort into dressing up, and I would later refer to her clothing choices as "prom clothes".

Every day that we were at Mara's house, Olivia came over, and each time, she'd gone out of her way to dress herself. Truthfully, she was extremely overdressed to be coming to someone's house just to hang out. I began to question Roger about her because I could feel something between them; something that felt too much like a soul tie, but how could that be? We were newlyweds and we were *supposed* to be in love.

Hard Head, Soft Behind

On the third day, Roger came to me and said that Mara had asked him to go to her son, Jacob's, university and speak with his professor on the following day. He said that she'd bought his train ticket and he'd be gone half of the day. This didn't make sense to me, so I questioned him and told him I would be coming along as well. I was tired of being cooped up in that apartment, especially considering it was mid-June and Mara didn't believe in turning on her air conditioner. She would even complain if we turned on a fan, and again, *we were in Atlanta, Georgia in mid-June.* Roger insisted that he go alone, even though I offered to buy my own train ticket. Of course, I was suspicious, but at the same time, I didn't want my past experiences with Taylor to influence my marriage to Roger. Roger told Mara I insisted on going with him, so she came into the room and insisted that I stay home with her. She said she wanted to teach me to cook African food; plus, she needed help with a few things. She said that Roger would only be gone a few hours and we could use that time for girl talk. Feeling double-

Hard Head, Soft Behind

teamed, I finally agreed.

The next day, I woke up to an empty bed. Roger had already left, so I got up, took a shower, and went into the living room. Mara didn't need help with anything after all; instead, when I offered to help her cook, she declined my help, so I laid down on the couch and popped a DVD into the DVD player. I was so into the movie, I didn't have time to really think about Roger's absence, but when the movie went off, I immediately noticed that Olivia hadn't come by that day. She'd been at Mara's apartment every day, spending almost the whole day with us while dressed in her "prom clothes", but now, she was missing, along with my husband. It didn't take me long to realize that I'd been set up, lied to, and disrespected in the worst way. I felt low; I felt stupid, and my self-perception immediately took a hit. How could I have married some man from another country who I'd met online? Why had I been so desperate that I'd allowed myself to become nothing more than a pawn in some sick game he and his sister were playing? I was ashamed of myself and how I'd carried myself as a woman who claimed to love the LORD. I couldn't contain my fears or my anger, and I made it known to Mara that I knew where Roger was and who he was with. Of course, Mara continued to lie and tried to make me feel bad about questioning her morals; nevertheless, I called Jacob's cell phone, and asked to speak with Roger. He said that the two of them were on a bus together and on their way back to the residence, but when I asked to speak with Roger, he said he was at the front of the bus and Roger was at the back of the bus. He said that he'd have him call me back. By this time, Mara had picked up her phone and started making calls, yelling at whomever was on the other end in their foreign tongue. The atmosphere was intense and my heart felt as if it had stopped beating. How could they do something so wicked to me? How could Roger cheat when we were still newly married? How could Mara invite me into her home, and then, distract me so Roger could go off and be with his mistress, girlfriend, wife, or

Hard Head, Soft Behind

whoever she was. My sister was off at one of her friend's houses, so I had no one there who was on my side.

Suddenly, my cell phone rang, and it was Roger. He was calling me from a strange number that he'd claimed belonged to a passenger on the bus he was on. I asked him why he hadn't called me from Jacob's phone, and he said that they were not on the same bus. Of course, this contradicted what Jacob had just told me moments earlier, so we argued. Thirty minutes after we'd hung up, Olivia suddenly showed up wearing a yellow dress and looking confused, but I was in no way deceived. I realized that Mara had instructed her to come over by herself in an attempt to throw me off, so her sudden appearance didn't make things better, especially since Roger had called back and was now on the other end saying he needed a ride back to his sister's place. Instead of sitting down, Olivia stood in the doorway looking as if she was waiting on Mara for instructions. She was clearly nervous and kept looking around. I went into the bedroom Roger and I had been sleeping in, and I began to pack my clothes. Olivia suddenly left and Mara called me into the dining room. "You don't trust me," she said with her very thick accent. "You think I would invite you here and send your husband to be with another woman? You're crazy if you think that!" Was I crazy? Had Taylor's repeated adulteries taken a toll on my ability to trust another man? No. I knew better. After having dealt with Taylor's adulteries for the seven years we were married, I was nothing short of a professional at knowing when I was being played. I looked at Mara in dismay. As cruel as some people can be, she'd just done one of the wickedest acts to me that could ever be done to another human being outside of touching them. I wanted to believe I was wrong; after all, I was still a newlywed. Needless to say, it didn't matter how hard I tried to believe her, I could not accept the lies she was speaking. Mara asked me to sit down so she could talk with me, and the next sentence out of her mouth only infuriated me more. "All men cheat!" she yelled. Initially, she'd been trying to convince me that Roger was not off with Olivia, but somehow, she'd veered off into a topic about all men being cheaters. "All men cheat," she screamed. "And if you don't accept that your husband will cheat on you, you will have a heart attack." I rebuked her repeatedly. "All men don't cheat," I responded. "And if your brother cheats on me, I'm going to divorce him. I just divorced one man for cheating on me, and I'm definitely not about to accept another one." My words began to infuriate Mara all the more. After all, she'd told me that in their culture, the younger women would accept the pearls of "wisdom" from the older women, but even though she was older than me, I refused to accept the *dusty* pearls (foolishness) she was offering me. After repeatedly telling me that all men cheated, and listening to me say otherwise, Mara suddenly rose to her feet in anger. "You're going to have a heart attack!" she screamed. "No, I won't," I responded. Mara stormed off, and before long, Roger arrived ready to battle with me. Olivia also came back over, and sat in the living room as Roger and I argued viciously in the bedroom we'd been sleeping in. Mara came into the room and tried to convince me, once again, that I was being paranoid. I couldn't take it. I was in a house surrounded by people who were obviously not for me, so I put on my shoes and went for a walk to calm myself down.

As I was walking, I felt lower than stupid. A once overly confident and extra picky woman had been reduced to a woman who'd entered a second marriage, only to be used and disrespected. I was nothing more than a pawn in their sick and twisted game and it was obvious. I felt unattractive all of a sudden. After all, in my mind, the only women who met and married foreign men, and let those men take advantage of them, were obviously unattractive women with low self-esteem. Of course, I found out the hard way that this foolish reasoning was not true. I had been a woman broken by life, and even more broken by a previous relationship. I hadn't let GOD heal my heart completely, and I'd leaned to my own understanding when it came to re-entering the dating world. I'd sinned against GOD yet again, and I felt that what I was going through was my just, but overly cruel, punishment. You would think I would have left, divorced Roger, and learned a lesson, but I didn't. *It was not my season to leave.* You see, there was a lesson in that marriage that GOD wanted me to get, a lesson that would keep me from sinning against HIM with my body and my soul ever again.

The days went by, and Roger and I argued all the more about Olivia. He passionately, and almost convincingly, reiterated to me that he had not been with Olivia, nor was he attracted to her. Mara kept coming into the room day after day to tell me how foolish it was for me to think they'd pull such an evil stunt. She'd even rebuked me around Olivia, saying, "You think everyone wants your husband? No one wants your man but you." At that, Olivia whispered, "Yes, no one wants your man." I was offended, but I didn't know what to say that would sound CHRIST-like. I was still very much so in my

Hard Head, Soft Behind

flesh. I'd made up my mind that I was going to fight someone before leaving there, but thank GOD, I didn't.

The day finally came for Roger to go back to Europe and me to head back to Mississippi. Before we'd left Mara's house to drop him off at the airport, he'd angrily tried to convince me to stay with Mara instead of temporarily moving to Germany with him, but staying with Mara was just not an option for me. Finally, Roger was on a plane heading back to Germany, and a month later, I moved to Germany to start our six month stay there. We'd talked months in advance and agreed that I would quit my job to move to Europe and I knew his request for me to stay with Mara had been inspired by Mara. After all, she'd tried to convince me to stay, but I'd repeatedly declined.

Once I arrived in Germany, the beauty of our new home distracted us from our constant bickering. We'd moved to Eberbach and lived in a mountainous region, surrounded by apple

Hard Head, Soft Behind

orchards and beautiful homes. It was absolutely breathtaking. At this point, I was convinced he'd cheated on me, but I was trying to force myself to believe otherwise, because the truth meant I really needed to leave that man, even though we were still newlyweds and we'd just begun our lives together. The lie afforded me the opportunity to stay with him and see if my dreams with him would come true. I kept trying to choose the lie, but the truth had chosen me, so I couldn't get around what I knew to be true.

Roger started work almost immediately, and we settled into our new routine. We talked a lot about the incident that had taken place at Mara's house, and he kept insisting he and Olivia had not been together, nor was he interested in her. "She's not even the type of woman I'd go for," he'd repeatedly said. "She's not pretty at all, nor is she educated; besides, she likes to use men for money."

One morning, the alarm went off and Roger got up and went to take a shower, but he left his cell phone in the room with me. I'd stayed up all night working on the Internet and hadn't noticed his phone until it rang. I looked at the caller I.D. and noticed Olivia's name and number. When I answered the phone, she immediately hung up. I was enraged, so I called her back, but she would not answer the phone. I left her a voice message telling her that if she could not speak to me, she'd better not call my husband anymore. When Roger got out of the shower, I told him about Olivia's call. He called her back, but she wouldn't answer her phone, so he called Mara and told her what had happened. Mara asked to speak with me and pretended to be absolutely infuriated by Olivia's behavior. "I don't know why she hung up in your face," exclaimed Mara. "Don't worry. I'm going to call and yell at her. I will tell her to never call Roger's phone again, so don't you worry." Mara called me several times that day to tell me that she'd yelled at Olivia and forbade her from ever calling Roger again. Again, I wasn't in the least bit thrown off; I was just trying to figure out what I should do that wouldn't involve me going back to

Hard Head, Soft Behind

my mother's house. I decided that if Mara was going to pretend to be on my side, I'd pretend to believe her, for the sake of keeping arguments down...at least for a little while.

While I was in Germany, my relationship with GOD continued to grow, and even though I didn't hear from Olivia for a long time, I knew I'd eventually have to face the truth and stop avoiding it. One day, while working on Roger's computer, I found a picture of Olivia wearing his coat. She was clearly in Germany, but he wasn't in the picture with her. *He was obviously the one taking the picture.* I then found the copy of an airline ticket he'd purchased for Olivia on his computer. He'd bought that ticket for her to come from Georgia to Germany just weeks before I'd arrived. I was so angry, I felt numb. When I confronted him, he said the jacket Olivia was wearing was not his, and he attempted to remind me that the manufacturer had made more than one of those jackets. In relation to the ticket, he said that she'd asked him to purchase the ticket for her because of some

Hard Head, Soft Behind

issues with her credit card. He told me that he'd done it as a favor, but hadn't seen her when she'd come to Germany. He insisted that she'd emailed him the picture of herself for reasons unknown, and that's how it had ended up on his computer. Even though I knew better, I decided to leave the situation alone yet again. I needed my peace and I was in a foreign country where I didn't know anyone. Besides, going back to my mother's house seemed just as bad as, if not worse than, the situation I was in. I felt as if I had nowhere to go and no one to turn to, so I turned to the LORD. Nevertheless, GOD was allowing me to get a lesson so powerful, it would not only change my life, but it would also change the minds of countless women from all around the world.

Fast forward to a year later. Roger and I were settling down in Florida and he'd just started working at the same company he'd worked with while writing his thesis in Germany. Mara and I weren't on speaking terms because I was absolutely disgusted with her ever-so-persistent

Hard Head, Soft Behind

attempts to control my husband and myself. I wanted no part of her, and by then, the feeling was definitely mutual. Nevertheless, Mara was an all-too-present force in our lives, calling Roger several times a day, every day. She told him what to do, how to dress, and how to treat me, and he followed through faithfully. I was a woman in agony, a woman stripped down to her bare faith, but better than that, I was a woman whose relationship with GOD had grown a lot stronger. I began to seek instruction from GOD daily, and HE began to grow me up at an alarming rate. HE did something that was so wonderful, yet it felt so cruel: HE filled all of my voids in the midst of that marriage. Additionally, HE handed me my earthly assignment. Suddenly, I felt complete and I often wondered why I was married in the first place. The man I was married to, in my mind, was nothing more than Mara's puppet, and I'd been the fool who'd paid for tickets to watch their show. GOD gave me a love for myself that I'd never experienced before. Suddenly, I felt beautiful again, and I was no longer ashamed of my testimony. Suddenly, I realized I was *too good* to be married to the man I was married to, but I knew I couldn't leave just yet. I wanted GOD to do whatever HE was planning to do in that marriage, and many times, I thought HE'D just change Roger and cause him to come clean about his relationship with Olivia. I was fully aware of the fact that GOD was going to use me to minister to HIS daughters and HE would use my testimony to minister to HIS hard-headed daughters. So, I stayed put, praying often, fasting whenever necessary, and seeking a greater knowledge and relationship with YAHWEH. The more I sought HIM, the more I found wisdom, and the more I found wisdom, the more I found my true identity (purpose) hidden in my FATHER'S heart.

One day, the truth about Roger and Olivia came to the light. I discovered Roger had a secret email account that I had no knowledge of because he'd changed the email address I had on my cell phone account to his own email address. I knew, however, that his password would likely be the common password he'd used to enter most of his accounts. *Let's face it, married women often know their husbands' passwords, even when their husbands are unaware of this fact.* I logged into his account, and the first thing I noticed was an email from someone using his brother's nickname. I opened the email, but it was in French. I forwarded the email to myself and downloaded the picture attached. The email was a few years old, but the photo told a story that would never expire. On the photo stood Olivia with Roger behind her. He had his arms wrapped around her waist and she'd placed her hands on top of his hands. It was obvious that they were a couple, but something else stood out. In the photo, Roger was clearly in Georgia wearing the exact clothes he'd worn the day he'd claimed he had to go to Jacob's university. Olivia, on the other hand, was wearing something other than the yellow dress I'd seen her in that day, but it was very clear that the photo had been taken on that exact day we'd fought about Olivia at Mara's house. I confronted him and he finally confessed to having been with

Hard Head, Soft Behind

Olivia that day, but insisted that nothing happened between them. He claimed Olivia was supposed to take him to the school, but he'd lied to me because Mara had told him to lie to protect my feelings. He said that Olivia had taken him back to her apartment, told him a long story about an engagement she'd had with another man some time ago, an engagement that had been terminated by her fiancé's mother. According to Roger, after pouring out her heart to him, Olivia had tried to get him to have sex with her. He said that he didn't have sex with her because he was wondering why her ex-fiancé's mother was against her son marrying Olivia; plus, he didn't want to hurt me. He admitted to being tempted, but claimed he couldn't follow through because of the story Olivia had told him. Roger then stood to his feet, grabbed my hands, and pleaded with me to believe him that nothing had happened between him and Olivia. By this time, there was no doubt left that he'd had an affair, and that the affair had lasted for years. The anger and hurt that welled up inside me was quickly snuffed out by a wave of peace, and I knew that peace was from the LORD. On one hand, I knew how I'd usually respond, but on the other hand, the desire to lash out just wasn't there.

I went and took the note Olivia had sent my husband through an online translating tool, and her words confirmed my worst fears. The note was a few years old, but in the note, she spoke of the day she'd spent with Roger and how she'd enjoyed watching one of Denzel's Washington's movies with him. She said that seeing how hurt he was watching Denzel's son in the hospital (on the movie, of course) had made her realize how great of a father he'd be to *their* children someday. She went on to say that she had missed a couple of periods, and if she were to hear the news that she was pregnant, it would be great news. Honestly, by this time, I was too wrapped up in GOD'S peace to feel anything besides disappointment. I was hurt, but the pain couldn't torment me. I was angry, but the anger couldn't consume me. Why hadn't I left when I'd initially seen this travesty unfolding? Why had I stayed year after year with a man who was clearly in a committed relationship with someone else? Again, the answer is as simple as it was complicated: *it wasn't my season to leave.* One part of me wanted to feel stupid, but GOD just wouldn't let me feel that way anymore. HE continued to instruct me day after day until that inevitable day arrived...the day Roger left. I'd overcome a merciless and unsympathetic strongman. I'd overcome a loveless marriage, and I'd come out of it sharpened and with a renewed mind. By this time, I'd grown up so much in the LORD that GOD was using me mightily, so Roger's departure was actually something I'd prayed for. I was grieved about the ending of our marriage at first, but at the same time, I was overwhelmingly relieved that it was finally over and I could start the healing process. I'd finally learned to love me with the love of GOD because I'd finally surrendered my whole heart to the LORD. Of course, I loved GOD so much more because I had a greater depth of knowledge about

Hard Head, Soft Behind

HIM, wisdom from HIM, and understanding about my storms. I wanted to just be alone with my FATHER and let HIM continue to change my mind. You see, when I was in the world, I had a confidence about myself that was nothing short of demonic. I hated myself so much, I became conceited; meaning, my self-confidence was purely built upon the opinions of others. Using that marriage, GOD had built me up with a confidence in HIM, and that confidence caused me to love me because HE loved me. The enemy wanted that marriage to tear me down, but GOD used it to build me up. I'd realized I deserved far better than the men I'd chosen for myself. I'd realized I am the daughter of the King of kings, and as such, only a HOLY SPIRIT filled man would be honored to have me as his wife. I realized GOD had already chosen my husband for me, but HE'D let me entertain the men I'd chosen for myself to teach me a much needed lesson. I was a student in the game of hard-knocks because GOD wanted to grow me up to be a teacher to the hard-headed. All the same, when

Hard Head, Soft Behind

you're anointed and hard-headed, sometimes your tests will reflect the size of your anointing.

The Revelation

After my first marriage ended, GOD could not give me the revelation I needed because I was not seeking the Kingdom of GOD and all HIS righteousness; therefore, everything else could not be added to me. I was still self-seeking and thought I could make GOD comply with my plans for myself. While married the second time, on the other hand, I was seeking GOD with such an intensity that GOD began to grow me up at an alarming rate. I watched myself die daily until I could no longer recognize my own reflection in the mirror. The girl looking back at me was beautiful and happy, even though she was in a dead end and demonically arranged marriage. It was then that GOD began to give me revelation because HE knew I was not the same woman I'd been a few years back, and HE knew I would never put myself or a man before HIM *ever* again. HE knew HE could trust me because I'd learned to finally trust HIM.

The Revelation

While married to Roger, I found myself questioning why I'd once felt so low that I'd allowed myself to stay with men who'd repeatedly and mercilessly abused my heart. Below is what GOD revealed to me:

- **My thinking had been generational.** The women (and men) in my family made idols out of the people they were romantically involved with, to the point where two of my uncles had been killed trying to hold on to adulterous women.
- **My love for myself wasn't real.** I didn't love GOD like I needed to love HIM, so it was impossible for me to love myself like I needed to love me. My love for me had been based on what others said to and of me and not what GOD said about me.
- **I tried to use men to repair myself.** Now, if you've read any of my books, you'll know that I'd grown up in a dysfunctional home, I'd been molested countless times as a child by countless people, and I'd never seen a real demonstration of true love.

The Revelation

Therefore, I didn't know the difference between love and lust. I tried to use men to fill all of the empty voids and heal all of the hurts that had been created in my life, and, of course, they couldn't heal or deliver me. Instead, they were imperfect human beings who needed just as much, if not more, deliverance and healing as I did.

- **I didn't know my own self-worth.**
Because I didn't know my own self-worth, I let men tell me how much I was worth (to them), and then, I began to depend on those "helpings" of love they portioned out to me day after day. Any time I realized I could lose the husband I had, I realized I could lose my source of self-worth. GOD started filling my voids and transforming my mind while I was married to Roger, and I immediately began to see life differently. I also began to grieve at the realization of how I'd hurt the LORD in my attempts to please myself.
- **I was trying to prove to others that I**

wasn't the failure they'd predicted I'd be. Now, this is where my dysfunctional family came in. While growing up, I'd been subjected to many hurtful words, and I'd come to understand that I was expected to fall and fail.

- **GOD had placed a call on my life and I was trying to figure out how to answer it.** When I was in the world, I felt that call; when I was in the church, I felt that call, but I didn't know the call was from GOD. I thought it was Mother Nature telling me to get a man.

- **The devil wanted to kill me, but GOD wanted to use me.** The enemy knew GOD would use me to minister to HIS daughters one day, so the enemy wanted to destroy my testimony. The enemy knew I was to be the helpmate to a powerful man of GOD one day, and he did everything he could to intercept that man while I was still in my broken state. Nevertheless, what he sent to kill me only gave me a testimony, and

The Revelation

> when GOD took the shame away, that testimony became a weapon against the enemy and his kingdom.

My time spent in the second marriage was time spent gaining the wisdom, knowledge, and understanding I needed to keep me over the course of my life. Those treasured blessings would not only build me up, but they tore down every lie the enemy had told me. Eventually, I became a woman who didn't *need* a man. I became a woman who walked around in the confidence and love of the LORD. I passionately and confidently declared I'd NEVER fornicate again, and I'd NEVER enter into a marriage with a man whom GOD didn't give permission to have my invaluable hand. I realized I am a treasured woman of GOD whose worth is far above rubies and gold.

Now, let's talk about you. You've likely seen yourself in me through at least one of my stories or thoughts. If you're married to an adulterous

The Revelation

man, you've picked up this book while in a dreadful state of oblivion. You're looking for answers, and you're either looking for a way out of that marriage or a reason to stay in it. Here's the truth: your husband commits adultery because he wants to commit adultery. Now, the word "wants" means "to desire", and this means he has not yet submitted himself to a changed mind. He's entertaining devilish thinking, and you're paying the price emotionally, socially, and financially for his choices. It feels unfair; I get that, but if I may sum this book up in a few words, this is what I can offer you: *he's doing what he wants to do. Now you have to ask yourself what you want to do about it.* You can't change him and you can't change his mind for him. You can follow him, check his cell phone records, yell at him, hit him, cry, threaten suicide, scream at his mistress, take him to church, put holy oil on his head while he's sleeping, or threaten to divorce him, but none of those things will be effective with a man who's willed it within his heart to commit adultery. You have to understand that his sin is first and

The Revelation

foremost against GOD, so before he changes, he'd have to repent, and to repent means to turn away from the sin altogether, being sorrowful about having participated in the sin. After repenting, he'd have to embrace a changed mind, otherwise, he'd find himself being led astray by his own dark and lustful desires yet again. You are not the issue, and adultery is not the root of your problems with him, idolatry is. When he placed himself before the LORD, he became his own idol, and therefore, he resorted to sacrificing his relationship with GOD, his marriage, his children's stability, and the life of the woman (or women) he's cheating with (fornication is a sin against one's self). He did this for the sake of quenching a deep and dark lust that had been formed through his idolatrous relationship with himself. To be selfish means to make an idol of one's self.

Instead of praying against his adulterous affairs and his mistresses, try binding idolatry. Instead of anointing your husband, begin to anoint your home. The reason for this is: your husband has free will, and he can do whatsoever he desires to do, even if his forehead is oily and his shoes have been prayed over. GOD does not and will not infringe upon a person's will. While anointing your home, decree and declare that the spirit of idolatry and the spirit of adultery cannot enter your house, and if they attempt to do so, command the angels GOD has assigned to you to arrest those demonic spirits, bind them, and cast them into the abyss until the day of Judgment. It sounds far-fetched, but you have the power to bind on earth and loose on earth.

Matthew 18:18: Verily I say unto you, whatsoever ye shall bind on earth shall be bound in heaven: and whatsoever ye shall loose on earth shall be loosed in heaven.

Please know that blessing your home will not guarantee your husband will stop his adulterous affair, but it will keep the enemy from entering your house *if you have faith.* When dealing with an adulterous spouse, the correct thing to do is go into spiritual warfare, rather than arguing with the spouse; after all, it's not what we see that's the problem. Oftentimes, it's what we don't see that poses the greatest threat to our marriages, our sanity, and every blessing GOD has reserved for us.

Ephesians 6:12: For we wrestle not against flesh and blood, but against principalities, against powers, against the rulers of the darkness of this world, against spiritual wickedness in high places.

The Shame

I don't know a woman alive who's suffered through an adulterous marriage and wasn't ashamed of her husband's indiscretions. Adultery doesn't give a woman the chance to endure the seven stages of grief privately; instead, adultery is oftentimes a very public deed. Some people will see a woman's husband out with his mistress, while others may hear about his philandering ways through mutual friends. For this reason, a woman who endures a marriage to an adulterous man has many emotions overwhelming her at any given time, and one of those emotions is humiliation. Being humiliated makes it a lot harder for the grieving wife to heal. Instead, she is often reminded of her husband's indiscretions any time someone looks at her sorrowfully or judgmentally. It also gives some people the idea that they have a right to voice their opinions about her decision to stay or leave.

The Shame

The words "humiliation" and "humble" are both derived from the word "human." To be humbled is to be reminded that you are human. To be humiliated is to be reminded that you are dirt. Enduring the pain of an adulterous affair is truly a humbling process, but enduring that pain publicly is humiliating. Not only does the wife have to deal with her own pain, but she also has to deal with the opinions of others; namely, those who are closest to her. All too often, insensitive or broken people become involved and want to rush her to make a decision that she needs more time to ponder. Many women try to leave their adulterous husbands vicariously through other women; meaning, they will encourage you to leave your husband, but remain with their own adulterous husbands. If you were to leave, they'd use your story as a warning shot to their husbands in their attempts to get them to stop "playing the fields". With adultery, a lot of people become involved, and this only intensifies the pain and causes the victim to feel rushed and defensive. Victims of adultery often live in a panicked state.

The Shame

After Taylor and I separated, I started being stopped by people who'd known us when we were together. They began to share stories of questionable or immoral things they'd seen Taylor doing when married to me. I was trying to heal and move on with my life, and for that reason, I avoided many public places. I even dreaded going to work. I hated the pitiful looks people gave me. I hated being pitied... period. My home life had been turned upside down, so I wanted some normalcy somewhere, but I couldn't seem to find a safe haven outside of church. At work, I watched the gossips flock together, and I knew when my name was on the menu. I didn't care about what they were saying. I was only upset that they were being insensitive to what I was going through. In public places, I dreaded seeing familiar faces, but living in a city with a population of just over 40,000 people made avoiding familiar faces almost impossible. Instead of going to the store to buy groceries, I would spend most of my time at fast food restaurants, sitting in the drive-thru. I became even more introverted than I was

The Shame

before in my attempts to protect myself from the vultures who were eager to peck the scabs off my healing heart. I wanted to heal in silence and in peace. I had a couple of friends who I hung around, but I stayed away from crowds as much as possible.

Even when I was with Taylor, I dealt with humiliation because one of his mistresses had called one of my co-workers and sent a message to me; a message she didn't tell me personally, but had spread around the office at my workplace. That message was, "Tell Tiffany I'm sleeping with her husband." The message had gotten back to me through another co-worker who I was friends with. She'd thought I'd heard about the message and called me to ask why I hadn't confided in her. I reassured her that I was not aware of the message, and I briefly ended the call so I could deal with the new revelation. I'd known about this mistress, and even though Taylor claimed there was nothing going on with them, I knew better. So, having to suddenly go into an office where I

The Shame

was being talked about, laughed at, and secretly mocked was almost as tormenting as staying with the man who'd started this domino effect.

Feeling ashamed is not only normal, but it's also healthy because it helps you to empathize with others who will eventually walk that same path you're on. Make no mistake about it, if you let GOD lead you, HE will call your tests a seed, plant them in HIS will, and cause you to birth a testimony that will help many people from around the world.

With Roger, I felt uttermost humiliation because I felt like I'd stepped pretty low to marry some man I'd met online and to have him do the things to me that he had done. I was really ashamed of the fact that he was cheating on me while we were still newlyweds. I didn't want people to see me as a desperate woman; after all, I was still battling with pride, and I felt like desperation was a huge fall away from my former confident self. Additionally, I'd left a marriage where I'd felt loved (when there

The Shame

was no other woman around), and I'd stepped all the way down, entering a loveless marriage where I was used and repeatedly mistreated. I felt lower than the lowest form of life on earth. Truthfully, if I had read my testimony and it had come from another woman, I'd think she had a severe case of low self-esteem and she was inexplicably desperate. But having to be the woman who'd experienced such a cruel game was surreal, and it was as humbling as it was humiliating.

When I stopped being ashamed about my testimony and my experiences, the enemy lost his power over me. You see, when the enemy is able to weigh you down with shame, he is able to control you with that shame. It won't be long before that humiliation becomes a fear. If you're feeling ashamed, try sharing your story with others, but not just random people. Share your story with women who can benefit from it. If you can't bring yourself to do this, ask the LORD to deliver you from the opinions of people and the cares of this world.

The Shame

Mark 4:18-19: And these are they which are sown among thorns; such as hear the word, and the cares of this world, and the deceitfulness of riches, and the lusts of other things entering in, choke the word, and it becometh unfruitful. And the cares of this world, and the deceitfulness of riches, and the lusts of other things entering in, choke the word, and it becometh unfruitful.

The Reason He Cheated

Most women want to know why their husbands cheated on them, and I've heard many women attempt to blame others for their husbands' adulterous affairs. One of the people often blamed is the mistress, and this, in itself, is error. There are millions, if not billions, of women in this world who'd give their bodies to your husband, and they aren't all prostitutes. There are millions of educated women who'd happily give your husband the time of his adulterous life. There are millions of religious women who hide behind their religious cloths after being between the sheets with someone's husband. The point is, there are just too many people in this world who you could be mad at, but why tear your soul into a million pieces trying to maintain a relationship with those people? Let's be real here. To be mad at someone, you have to have a direct or indirect relationship with that person because that person will be in your heart and thoughts until you forgive

The Reason He Cheated

them. It's not her fault that he did what he did. Sure, it's upsetting to see a woman participate in the destruction of another woman, but the truth is, there is no such thing as a whole mistress. She's broken, so she's looking to have her voids (or wallet) filled.

Why did your husband cheat? Was it because you'd gained weight? Was it because he was no longer attracted to you? Was it because things had "leveled off" between the two of you, and he'd become bored? No. Your husband cheated because he wanted to. That's the lesson so many women refuse to accept because in realizing they are not at fault, they are forced to come to the reality that their husbands are selfish, immoral, and ungodly; that is, until they have repented, of course. If they were to come to this reality, they'd be forced to choose between staying with those men, knowing full well what they were, or leaving. For most women, it's easier to bear some of the blame than it is to just accept that their husbands just refuse to be monogamous. For some women,

The Reason He Cheated

it's easier to blame the mistress than it is to accept that if the husband had not been willing, there would be no mistress. The only time that a wife could bear some of the blame for her husband's adulterous affairs is when she has repeatedly refrained from giving herself to him sexually, and because I know that statement would infuriate some people, let me back it up with scripture.
1 Corinthians 7:5: Defraud ye not one the other, except it be with consent for a time, that ye may give yourselves to fasting and prayer; and come together again, <u>that Satan tempt you not for your incontinency</u>.

The word "incontinency" means "incontinence" in modern day English, and Merriam-Webster defines "incontinence" as *failure to restrain sexual appetite.*
We are creatures who like to have sex, and a married man becomes used to having sex with his wife. If you start withholding your body from him, he may feel unloved, unwanted, and out of control. Of course, some other woman would be more

than willing to help him feel loved, wanted, and in control yet again. The Bible tells us that Satan will tempt us through our incontinence. The Bible also tells us that our flesh is weak.

Matthew 26:41: Watch and pray, that ye enter not into temptation: the spirit indeed is willing, but the flesh is weak.

Of course, most men will blame their wives for their adulterous affairs. They do this because they don't want to bear the full blame. It's not that they truly feel their wives are responsible for their choices. They simply don't want to feel that they are at the mercy of their wives. In sharing the blame with their wives, they know their wives will likely stay a little longer and work a little harder at those marriages. This buys them enough time to choose which route they want to go, and for the men who are determined to make their marriages work, this buys them enough time to work at keeping their marriages together. If they can convince their wives that they are somewhat to blame, or fully at fault, they could keep their wives

The Reason He Cheated

from gaining access to the power they so dread losing. What is this power? The power to make an informed decision without feeling any kind of guilt. It would be all too easy for a woman to walk away from a man she's given her all to if she were to realize that her all wasn't enough for him. You see, if you were to suddenly realize that you are a great woman and wife, your husband would feel that he was at your mercy and most men don't like to feel that way. If you were to realize you are not to blame, and some other man would be more than happy to be a faithful husband to you, your shattered confidence would begin to mend itself. If you were to realize you are as beautiful as GOD created you to be, you'd seek the LORD to make you whole again, and this wholeness would prove to be a threat to your broken husband.

Some of the most common excuses men give for their adulterous affairs are:
- You argue too much. I got tired of arguing.
- It happened when I was mad at you. I wasn't thinking.

The Reason He Cheated

- You and I had argued, I left, and I hadn't planned to come back. I thought you and I were finished.
- She came on to me, and in my moment of weakness, I fell.
- The passion between us has fizzled out.
- I'm a man.
- It was an accident.
- You've changed.
- I was tired of the same old thing. I wanted to try something new.
- It was just sex, nothing else.

Whatever your husband's reason for cheating, please know that you are not to blame. He has free will, and an ongoing adulterous affair is fully premeditated.

- It requires that the adulterous duo meet up, and during the drive, both parties have plenty of time to think about what they are doing and what they are going to do. This is an act of premeditation, of course.
- It requires the couple to speak regularly.

The Reason He Cheated

Please know that there aren't many women who will meet a man at a hotel, have sex with him, and leave without any communication. Most women who do this are seasoned prostitutes.

- It requires the man to flatter the woman, in most cases. In other words, it requires a lot of thinking on his part.
- It requires a lot of planning. The husband has to know his wife's work schedule, her whereabouts at any given time, and the areas she's likely to drive through. He'll intentionally avoid those areas unless his mistress lives in one of those areas. In this case, he'd have to take extra precaution to hide his vehicle any time he visits her.
- It requires money, in many cases. Many adulteresses want something out of those relationships outside of sex and promises that they will one day be in the wife's shoes. And most men know exactly what to give them, and that's money or gifts. By giving the mistresses something of value (besides

their DNA), the husbands send a message to their mistresses that they are valuable to them.
- It requires that the duo remove their clothes, and again, this is an act of premeditation.
- Finally, they can repent and stop their affair, but an ongoing relationship means they didn't want to stop.

I know many women are looking for some super-deep reasons as to why their husbands committed adultery, but there are none. The real reasons *some* men cheat include:
- They weren't in a solid relationship with GOD.
- They'd made idols of themselves.
- They did not love their wives as they loved themselves, which is against the WORD of GOD.
- They hadn't cast down evil imaginations and every high thing that exalted itself against the knowledge of GOD.

The Reason He Cheated

- They loved the lie more than they loved the truth.
- They weren't ready to be married when they married because they weren't in a fully committed relationship with the LORD.
- They were the victims of generational thinking; meaning, their fathers likely committed adultery against their mothers. Adultery is a generational curse or stronghold that runs through their families.
- Their wives were refraining from sex with them. *(That's the hard truth).*
- They were cheaters when their wives married them, but those women married them thinking they could change them.
- They were taught that all men cheated, and therefore, based their manhood on their abilities to carry on extramarital relationships.
- They wanted to cheat.

Of course, there are more reasons that are not listed, but many of those reasons would fall under

The Reason He Cheated

the categories above. The lesson is, if a man wants to cheat, he will do just that.

Before I discovered Taylor's adulteries, I thought I was the perfect wife. I'd done everything society (and Hollywood) said a wife ought to do to keep her husband. I thought there was no way he would cheat on me because he wasn't lacking anything. After he'd confessed to his affairs, I had many questions, and one of those questions was why he'd cheated. After all, when he wasn't cheating, we were best friends. I didn't understand what could possibly make him want to go outside of me. He looked at me and shrugged his shoulders, and finally, he said (paraphrased), "I don't know. It's not that I wasn't happy at home. Truthfully, many times, I asked myself why I did it, but honestly, it was just something different. None of those women were better than you, and that's why I questioned myself many times, but there was a thrill in doing something you know you shouldn't be doing. It was stupid, I know, but that's the truth."

Is He Cheating?

Most women want to know the signs that their spouses are cheating, and for this reason, articles about adulterous men and the signs they are cheating have become very popular. This chapter is probably going to be the shortest chapter in this book because the answer is as plain as the nose on your face. If you think he's cheating, if your alarms are going off from within, then he's likely having an affair. I'll never forget hearing a statement from a private investigator on television. He said that 90% of women who suspect their husbands are cheating are right. They simply want their husbands to be caught. Now, I know that 90% of the women who read this statement are going to hope to GOD they are in that 10% who are wrong, but let me share something with you I learned while married the first time.
GOD put an alarm on the inside of a woman, and that alarm goes off any time her husband joins himself to another woman. Every time I suspected

Is He Cheating?

Taylor was cheating, I was right. Everything within me screamed that he was cheating, but I wanted to believe his words instead of the voice within. Little did he know, the words he'd spoken were not confirmed by GOD; instead, the more he spoke, the more I realized he was not being honest with me. When I tried to ignore the truth to believe my husband, I lost my peace because I'd become double-minded, and therefore, I became unstable. So, I couldn't leave the situation alone. I kept questioning him time after time, hoping he'd confess his affairs, repent of his affairs, and I could make an informed decision from there. Nevertheless, he insisted I was losing my mind, and was destroying our marriage with my insecurities and accusations. I then began to question myself, but the finger of blame kept turning back to him.

Of course, there are signs to look for that usually indicate adultery is taking place, and these signs include, but are not limited to:
- **He suddenly wants to update his**

wardrobe. Cheating men oftentimes give themselves away when they start showing more than a usual interest in their wardrobe and external appearance.

- **He suddenly needs new underwear.** Let's face it. Adulterous affairs are mainly just sex...nothing more, nothing less. For this reason, a wandering husband will want to look his best in the clothes his mistress sees him wearing the most: his underwear.
- **He suddenly starts wearing cologne or aftershave.** A lot of men start courting their mistresses in the same way they'd courted their wives. They go out of their way to impress them, but get this: In most cases, the man has no intention of spending his life with the mistress. His desire to drench himself in Old Spice is likely nothing less than a mating call.
- **He suddenly wants to change the soap he uses to bathe.** There are two main reasons he'd request this. First and foremost, he wants to smell heavenly to his

Is He Cheating?

mistress. Soap, to him, is his back-up cologne. And secondly, men often change the soap at home and start buying the same brand of soap their mistresses use. They do this because some men bathe at their mistress's houses after their sexual rendezvouses together. But coming home smelling like Irish Springs when you only have Dove at home is a cut and dry giveaway. So, many men will try to throw off the scent of their adulteries by changing the soap at home to match the soap their adulteresses' use.

- **He's suddenly independent and wants to be alone a lot.** Before the affair started, he was likely very much into you, and wanted to spend every waking moment in your presence, but after the affair started, he became elusive. There are several reasons for this, which include: (1). He feels guilty and wants to spend as little personal time with you as possible, (2). He wants some alone time so he can call his mistress, (3).

Is He Cheating?

He wants some alone time so he can rethink his decision to commit adultery, (4). He wants some alone time to mentally revisit his sexual encounters with the adulteress. This is purely an act of lustful perversion. And finally, (5). He knows you're on to him and does not want to answer any random questions.

- **He becomes verbally abusive.** Many men start feeling guilty about their affairs, and to compensate for how they feel, they begin to tear their wives down with their words. Additionally, some men become verbally abusive because to entertain their mistresses, they felt the need to speak reproachfully about their wives. While speaking of their wives in an unflattering way, many men have talked themselves into being angry with their wives for their past offenses. This is nothing more than an attempt to justify one's own behavior.
- **He becomes physically abusive.** Physical abuse is usually a fear tactic to

scare his wife into staying with him. He wants to tear down her self-worth and get her to fully and idolatrously depend on him for affection; that way, if she is to discover his indiscretions, she'd be too broken or scared to leave.

- **He looks for fault in you.** Many men look for fault in their wives in their attempts to justify having the affairs they are currently entangled in. They want to justify their choices, not only to their wives, but also to themselves, because even the cruelest man has some shred of a heart left.
- **He magnifies any small mistake you make.** This act is done out of pure desperation and selfishness. Men who do this often do so with the intent of making their wives feel like they are being lousy wives. This prepares the wife for the impact she'll feel once she discovers her husband's infidelities. By making her feel as if she were failing as a wife, he can elbow some of the blame to her once the

truth is revealed.

- **He's suddenly abnormally nice to you.** Now, this may baffle some, but many men treat their wives like royalty when they start having affairs. This is done because they feel guilty about what they're doing. I became suspicious of Taylor's after-work activities when he'd surprised me with a bracelet, necklace, and a plant. Even though gift-giving was nothing new in our household, there was something off about his behavior and his sudden choice to buy me a gift. Less than three days later, I discovered the first mistress, and she'd eventually told me that she'd helped him pick out the plant he'd purchased for me.
- **His sex drive changes.** Men engaging in adulterous affairs are usually burning themselves out with their mistresses; all the while, trying to build up enough strength to give their wives their due diligence. In other words, with his mistress, he's potent, but with his wife, he's impotent. This has

absolutely nothing to do with the wife and has everything to do with the fact that he wasn't designed to maintain multiple relationships. All the same, some men become extremely interested in sex once they start engaging in adultery. Believe it or not, the reason for this behavior is often guilt. Many men try to wash their guilt away by repeatedly having sex with their wives. This is also done to convince the wife that there is no way he (the husband) could be cheating.

- **His sexual personality changes.** Every man has a sexual personality, and once you're married, you will learn your husband's sexual personality and how he communicates sexually. The two of you will develop a sexual relationship with one another, where you'll become understanding toward one another's needs (unless one of you is extremely self-centered). You will know his bedroom language and he will know yours, but when

Is He Cheating?

he starts speaking another language, it's likely he learned it from someone who spoke that language. For example, sex between the two of you could have been slow and passionate previously, but all of a sudden, sex becomes merciless and dull.

- **He starts staying late after work.** Remember, the mistress wants quality time, too, and the wandering husband wants to do whatever he feels is necessary to get her in the position he wants her in, and most of the time, this position is lying down.

- **He starts riding or walking through certain neighborhoods.** You're in the car with your husband, and you notice that he's starting to take the long way home. This is oftentimes a sign that he's passing by some woman's house to check in on her. Example: Taylor and I had started going for long walks with our dog, but I noticed that the walks started getting longer and longer. I questioned why he wanted to go so far away from the house, but he said he just felt like walking. We'd walked through a particular neighborhood on two or three separate occasions, and I watched him as his head kept turning toward one of the streets we were passing by. I eventually found out that one of his mistresses lived on that street and we'd passed her house a few times while walking and many times while driving.

- **He asks for short separations, rather than a divorce.** I can't reiterate this enough. Most men who are involved in adulterous affairs have absolutely no plans to leave their wives...ever! They simply "want their cake and eat it, too". But when the fights between an adulterous man and his wife begins to escalate, many adulterers will request short separations. Contrary to popular belief, they don't always request to separate from their wives so they can spend every waking moment with their mistresses. In most cases, this is done by a man who feels cornered, a man who feels

Is He Cheating?

his wife is too hot on his adulterous trail. He's afraid that if he continues living with his wife, his indiscretions will be found out and he will lose his wife forever. By separating from her, he feels he can control the situation from afar, and figure out what he wants to do next. Before Roger filed for divorce, he asked me if we could separate for six months, but I said no. If we were going to be separate, it would be because we were divorcing, not taking a break. Short separations give men time to justify having affairs, and this tactic is often used by men who've discovered their mistresses are pregnant. In their attempts to save their marriages, they request a separation, with the intent of reconciling with their wives and blaming their outside children on the separation.

- **He becomes increasingly suspicious about you, even though your routine has not changed and you haven't given him any reason to question you.** Cheating men often become paranoid because they're afraid their wives could cheat on them. This paranoia is the result of guilt and an attempt to justify their own indiscretions. Additionally, in many cases, this guilt-trip is designed to make a woman feel as if her behavior is questionable. Her husband knows that by doing this, she will do everything possible to prove she's faithful, and this includes: Coming straight home from work, shortening her time with family and friends, and being hasty when running errands. In this case, the husband is simply trying to imprison his wife with guilt so she'll spend most of her time at home, while he is out with the mistress. This is an attempt to distract the wife and keep her from accidentally, or intentionally, stumbling across his secret.

- **Suddenly, he has a problem with a friend of yours or someone in your family.** Cheaters often try to separate their wives from their loved ones because they don't

Is He Cheating?

want their wives to have anyone to turn to once their secrets come to light. Not only do they attempt to separate their wives from family members, but in most cases, they will also try to breed contempt between their wives and their wives' families and friends. They want full control over their wives' decisions, and they want to make sure there is no one around to build them up after they've begun to tear them down. This truth may seem cruel, but it's real.

- **Your coupled friends start staying away.** In many cases, men will share their secrets with other men because they think those men are like themselves, when that's not always the case. Those men will, in turn, tell their wives about their friend's revelation. From there, the wife requests that the two of them stay away from the adulterous man and his wife, out of fear her husband will catch the adultery bug. If the man hasn't told his wife, the couple may

Is He Cheating?

have stumbled upon the adulterous man and his mistress somewhere, or they may have heard about his indiscretions from his wife or a mutual friend of the mistress.

There are many signs that a husband is cheating, but every wife knows her husband. She knows how he normally treats her, she knows his sexual personality, and she knows his routines. When any of these things are disturbed, it can be a sign that another woman (or man these days) has entered the picture.

Emotional Versus Physical Adultery

I think most women will agree that an emotional affair can be just as bad, if not worse, than a physical affair. That's because a man who involves himself emotionally with another woman isn't just opening his zipper for her, he's opening his heart to her. He's giving away a piece of himself that is sacred, and this usually means the affair isn't just a sexual affair, it's a blossoming relationship. Nevertheless, the average adulterous affair is mainly about sex for the husband, but that's not always the case with the mistress. For the husband, the mistress's house provides an oasis away from his reality. It is a temporary vacation spot where he can go and live life as a single man, all the while, enjoying the forbidden fruit that is another woman. After he's had his fill of the mistress for that day, he can return home to the reality and life he's worked so hard to establish. Because he didn't work for the mistress, he will likely never respect, love, or desire a long term commitment with her.

Most men who pursue physical relationships with other women do so because they want the adrenaline rush or high associated with doing something wrong. To them, it spices up their lives and rekindles a spark in them that they feel monogamy has stolen from them. In many cases, the other woman is nothing more than sexual therapy, an opportunity to explore what they feel they're missing out on. She's also an opportunity for them to discover how they really feel about their wives. Many husbands come to realize that their wives are invaluable to them once the threat of losing those wives surfaces. For this reason, many adulterous husbands will persistently, aggressively, and sometimes violently try to keep their wives from discovering their affairs. Many men who've struck their wives did so for the first time after they'd become entangled in their first adulterous affair. They were dealing with many emotions and fears, and striking their wives, to

Emotional Versus Physical Adultery

them, seemed like a logical response to all of the voices of reason going off within them and their wives' voices going off about them. It is very common for a first time adulterer to underestimate the weight of an affair. It is for this reason that an adulterer can be rather dangerous to his wife, his mistress, and himself.

Most men who pursue emotional affairs do so because of unresolved issues they have at home with their wives or in their workplaces. An emotional affair usually starts off as a friendship, where the adulterer and adulteress begin to confide in one another. Such behavior is dangerous because both parties open their hearts to one another, and the Bible specifically tells us to guard our hearts, for out of it pours the issues of life. A man who does not guard his heart will easily fall into the snares of a seductress. That's because most men don't understand that women think differently than men. Most men don't understand that a woman can be nice, helpful, intelligent, down to earth, and confident, and still

Emotional Versus Physical Adultery

be conniving. An adulteress who opens herself to be a friend can easily be mistaken for a decent woman. She can easily gain the trust and respect of the man she's coaching or speaking to because he may feel comfortable telling her things that he's uncomfortable telling his wife or anyone else, for that matter. All the same, it's easy for a man to enter an emotional affair with a woman when tensions are high at home. Initially, his relationship to the mistress was nothing more than two people discussing their issues, but after a few meaningful conversations, their communion blossomed into a budding relationship. In such cases, both parties may have foolishly and unintentionally opened their hearts to one another, and somehow, the enemy got in and was able to convince them that they were perfect for one another. Additionally, there are many crafty women out there who purposely open their hearts and ears to the husbands of other women with the intent of initiating affairs with those men. They are great listeners, they're very intelligent, and they appear to be everything a man wants in a wife.

Emotional Versus Physical Adultery

That's because a seductress isn't just a naïve woman who slips and falls into the bed with a married man, a seductress is a woman who's purposed in leading men astray. To do this, a seductress has to be very crafty and manipulative. She must also study her intended prey to get a better understanding of who he is and what he wants before she can successfully launch an effective campaign against his marriage. A seductress loves to hear a man talk about the problems he has with his wife, because it gives her the information she needs to customize her campaign (attack) against his marriage. A seductress will:

8. Listen intently to a man talk about his wife.
9. Listen for signs of entitlement. She listens for what he feels he's not getting from his wife, so she can offer it to him.
10. Pretend to side with the wife on a few issues so her intentions aren't so obvious.
11. Offer to speak with or befriend the wife. This is her attempt to size up her competitor. This is also her attempt to

Emotional Versus Physical Adultery

make the wife look insecure in the husband's eyes because most wives will discern the seductress's intentions, and will blatantly refuse to deal with her. This will often lead to an altercation between the husband and the wife, because the husband may see his wife's response as rude and humiliating. He may then attempt to console the seductress, all the while, bashing his wife for not opening her home or heart to the other woman.

12. Open their hearts and play the damsel in distress for their intended prey. Let's get one thing straight. A seductress is led by a demonic spirit, and as such, she's very crafty and she's skilled at destroying marriages. She's not always obvious, and for this reason, many men become entangled in her web of deceit. A seductress will tell a man about her problems and pretend to be clueless and overwhelmed because she understands that the man's natural instinct to defend or

Emotional Versus Physical Adultery

rescue a damsel will kick in. She will play on his inability to trust his wife's discernment.

You'll notice that in this chapter, I'm referring to the adulteress as a seductress, and there's a reason for this. We know that an adulteress is a woman who commits adultery, whether she be a wife or the other woman. A seductress, however, is more so the description of a crafty adulteress, a woman who's skilled at destroying relationships by tailoring her conversations and needs to a man's voids. Most seductresses don't just pursue physical relationships with married men, they pursue emotional relationships with married men. The enemy loves to see a man joining himself through sex with another woman, but once that man opens his heart to that other woman, the enemy sees a greater opportunity to not only destroy that man's marriage, but to also destroy him. That's what happened to Samson when he married Delilah. Samson engaged himself emotionally and physically with a woman who

Emotional Versus Physical Adultery

manipulated and exposed him to his enemy. It's safe to say that most, if not all, seductresses are led or possessed by what is commonly referred to as a Delilah spirit.

But what should you do if you suspect (or know) that your husband is involved emotionally with another woman? Below are ten tips to help you conquer Delilah:

11. Talk with your husband and tell him the ways of a crafty woman. All too often, men are naïve in relation to women, and may easily open themselves up to crafty and manipulative souls. Sometimes, talking with a man and informing him of what he's dealing with is enough to make him take a second look.
12. Talk with a few women who he trusts and respects, women who are moral and truthful. Sometimes, men have trouble receiving the truth from their wives in relation to other women because they think their wives' rants are rooted in insecurity.

Emotional Versus Physical Adultery

When a man hears from someone he respects, such as his mother or pastor's wife, he'll likely listen more intently to what's being said because he understands they have no motive.

13. Set up boundaries with your husband. Be sure to talk with your husband and tell him that you are not okay with him engaging any further with the other woman, and bring a solution to him. Men listen better when we bring solutions to the table, instead of problems. Draw up a short list of what you'd like for him, and make sure you present the conversation and list to him in love. Don't make demands as you may offend him. Instead, let him know that you love him and are simply protecting your family.

14. Speak with your husband more about whatever he wants to talk about. Sure, you may hate sports, but the mistress may pretend to like them, or she just may actually like them. This gives her common

Emotional Versus Physical Adultery

ground with your husband. The two of you should involve yourselves in one another's hobbies. At the same time, never make your husband feel as if he can't discuss certain things with you. Keep offense out of your conversations and simply learn to be friends as well as lovers.

15. Attend many Christian relationship workshops together. Because the two of you are familiar with one another and you've seen each other's flaws, it may be difficult for you to set rules and boundaries you both respect and honor. For this reason, some Christian marriage workshops may provide the two of you with a neutral environment where you can discuss your issues with a pastor or a Christian counselor.

16. Kill repetition. It's easy for a man or woman to grow tired when their lives are repetitive. Additionally, it's easy for a relationship to be strained when one or both parties begin to take one another for granted, and stop

doing fun things with one another. Be spontaneous. Be your husband's best friend, not just his wife. Remember this: Men tend to tell their best friends more than they tell their wives.

17. Compromise more. As women, we oftentimes become prideful and think we're always right, and such thinking can cause our husbands to lose respect for us. Marriage isn't about being right. Sometimes, you have to compromise with your husband so that he will feel appreciated and loved as opposed to feeling taken for granted. For example, if you want to go to Paris for the holidays, but your husband wants to go to Spain, the best thing to do is to be fair about it. Who picked the destination of your last trip? If it was you, be fair and let your husband choose this one.

18. Argue less. One of the greatest lessons I learned was that one can be right and still be wrong. How so? If you engage in an

Emotional Versus Physical Adultery

argument with your husband, you're wrong. You're just as wrong as he is because the two of you are not respecting one another's wishes. Sometimes, the best response is to simply support your husband, even when you don't support his decisions and vice versa. If he's wrong, one of the greatest lessons he'll ever get is finding out that he was wrong the hard way. This teaches him to trust you more, and it also makes him stronger and wiser. For example, if your husband wants to invest in some real estate and you know the property he is looking at isn't a great deal, tell him the truth. If he becomes offended and argumentative, don't stand in the way of him buying the property. If you're right and he's wrong, he will eventually learn an expensive lesson.

19. Stop trying to physically stop an affair from occurring, and start fighting in the spirit. A seductress is designed to attack men while pleasuring them. Pray against the spirits of

Emotional Versus Physical Adultery

idolatry, adultery and seduction, and continue to stand in the gap for your husband, even when he doesn't understand your stance. Understand that when the enemy sends a weapon out against your husband, that weapon is against you, too. Your husband needs you to fight (spiritually) for him, not against him.

20. Understand that the other woman is possibly not a seductress. She can be as naïve as your husband and end up falling into temptation with him. Don't oppose or befriend her. Instead, warn your husband, all the while, continuing to show love to her.

Physical affairs can transition into emotional affairs, especially when the couple has been physically involved for quite some time. Nevertheless, the only thing you can do as a wife is continue to pray for your husband, with your husband, and against the enemy (Satan). Also, pray for the other woman's healing and deliverance. Additionally, seek new knowledge

Emotional Versus Physical Adultery

and revelation along with your husband so the two of you can be aware of the wiles of the enemy. The more knowledge you seek, the more understanding you'll have, and the less problems you'll face.

What Adultery Does to Women

One of the amazing things about being a woman is, we are built to survive one of the greatest pains known to man: childbirth. After we've been ripped (or cut) wide open, we can expect an almost full recovery six to eight weeks after the child is born. But we were not designed to weather an adulterous spouse. Adultery was never supposed to be a part of life's equation, but, of course, sin brought it in. Unlike childbirth, adultery rips a woman's heart open, and it takes a lot more than six to eight weeks for her to fully recover. Some women have spent their lifetimes nursing the wounds brought on by their husbands' infidelities. Of course, as women of GOD, we know we have to forgive our spouses, regardless of whether we choose to stay with them or not.

Most men who participate in adultery have no clue what their selfish acts will do to their marriages,

What Adultery Does to Women

nor what it will do to their wives. That's because adultery is an act of selfishness, and selfish people have trouble empathizing with others. Many times, they have to experience hardships firsthand before they learn to be empathetic. But women who are being victimized by adulterous husbands and their ever-so-persistent mistresses will often try to find ways to help their husbands understand the magnitude of their adulterous acts. They do this by crying, trying to reason with their husbands, trying to educate their husbands about the ways of women who avail themselves to be mistresses, threatening to divorce their husbands, threatening to physically harm or destroy their husbands, or threatening to kill themselves. These acts of desperation are not only common, but they signal that the victim is beginning to think irrationally. But why do women become emotionally unstable when their husbands cheat? Below are 15 things that happen to a woman when she's being tormented by adultery.

1. **She becomes double-minded and**

unstable. Sure, she sees and understands what's going on around her, but because she's been lied to so much by her husband, she doesn't know what to believe anymore. On one hand, she can hear the truth ringing from within the depths of her soul, and on the other hand, she has her husband's words to consider. This causes her to become unstable.

2. **She starts to doubt GOD.** That little voice ringing from within, of course, is GOD. But an adulterous man will work overtime to get his wife to believe his words and to ignore the voice from within. After doubting GOD, she begins to lean toward her husband's words, and this can prove to be dangerous for him, because she's no longer listening to the voice of reason. A woman who's tuned GOD out is a danger to her husband, herself, and anyone else around her.

3. **She starts to live life reactively instead of actively.** When a woman is currently married to an adulterous man, her heart is

What Adultery Does to Women

not only broken, but it also becomes unguarded. Because her heart is unguarded, many dark and demonic thoughts can enter her heart, and she becomes overly sensitive. Instead of just living, she starts reacting to everything that nudges up against her heart, even her own children. That's because she's living life in a panicked state.

4. **She starts to lean on people she wouldn't ordinarily associate with.** In many cases, the people she begins to lean on are broken souls who are unapologetically sinful. That's because, in her pain, she can relate to them and they can relate to her. Of course, such behavior can put her in danger.

5. **She becomes increasingly distracted.** Problems in a marriage are often so hurtful, they can become distracting. Women married to adulterers are often very distracted because they're mentally revisiting conversations and searching for

What Adultery Does to Women

overlooked clues. This makes them prone to making careless mistakes at work, thus putting their jobs in jeopardy. This also makes them prone to accidents.

6. **She loses her peace.** You have to understand that a woman who's lost her peace will often retreat to her thoughts and other devices (phone checking, email hacking, and so on) in an attempt to retrieve her peace. She knows the only way this can be done is if she can get her husband's words to finally match up with what she's hearing from within. Nevertheless, she knows the voice within won't change, so she'll repeatedly question her husband in an attempt to finally get him to tell the truth.

7. **She becomes edgy.** You have to understand that she's lost her peace, so she's going to be extra moody. At the same time, adulterers usually justify their adulteries once their wives become cranky.

8. **She loses her ability to be a good wife**

and a good mother. At this time, she has to completely depend on the instruction of GOD because of all the mental warfare she's in. She's emotional, distracted, moody, and trying to nurture a broken heart; all the while, trying to fulfill her daily responsibilities. That's too much for one person, so a woman who's been broken has to utterly and completely walk by faith, otherwise, she can't possibly be a good wife and mother. She'll do her best, but because she's forgetful and distracted, she will skip many steps and make many mistakes.

9. **She becomes increasingly depressed.** Depression is often the result of purpose suppressed; meaning, because of what she's going through, she's not operating in her GOD-assigned purpose. This ultimately leads to depression, and depression can lead her down many dark roads.

10. **She loses respect for her husband.** One of the things GOD commands wives to do

What Adultery Does to Women

is to reverence, or respect their husbands, but a husband who's disrespecting his wife will often find himself losing the respect of his wife. Once a woman loses respect for her husband, she loses her ability to submit to and trust him. Submission and trust are vital for the survival of a Godly marriage.

11. **She ends up with secret enemies, and this places her in harm's way any time she leaves the house.** In most cases where adultery is factor in someone's marriage, the mistress knows who the wife is, but the wife does not know who the mistress is. It is not uncommon for a mistress to stalk and attack an unsuspecting wife, and, of course, there have been cases where women have been killed by their husbands' mistresses. Even when the wife is aware of the mistress and her identity, she will still find herself having enemies she knows nothing of.

Remember, the mistress has friends and family members, many of who will side with her and fight on her behalf.

12. **Her self-esteem is brought pretty low.** A single woman gets her self-perception from all of the single men who flirt with her, but a wife usually sees herself through her husband's eyes. If her husband commits adultery, she will likely believe her appearance has something to do with it. So, it is not uncommon for the wives of adulterous men to repeatedly change their appearances. They may dye or cut their hair, and in many cases, women will often change their hairstyles altogether. This is done in an attempt to get their husbands' attention.

13. **The sun often sets on her wrath.** This causes her to walk in unforgiveness, and often, away from the blessings of GOD.

14. **She starts entertaining the thoughts of or maybe even practicing witchcraft unknowingly.** Let's face it. Manipulation is witchcraft, and a woman whose husband has exposed her to adultery will often resort

to using manipulation and other devices in an attempt to flush out the truth.

15. **She starts being tempted by the same adulterous spirit that has charmed her husband.** When a woman is emotionally starved, deprived of affection, craving attention, and spiritually exposed, adultery starts looking like a beautiful hero riding in on a white house. As with my case, my initial decision to commit adultery against Taylor was done purely out of retaliation, but it immediately blossomed into an addiction. I thought I needed the other guy to feel loved and desired. All the same, I felt as if Taylor and his mistresses were teamed up against me, so having another guy made me feel like I had someone on my side.

Of course, the list above displays some of the things or mindsets many women wrestle with when their spouses are involved in extramarital affairs, but the point is, adultery makes a huge

What Adultery Does to Women

impact on a woman's mind, soul, and life, and this is why we must, at all times, be led by the HOLY SPIRIT of GOD.

If you are a wife married to a two-timing husband, please know that you absolutely have to depend on GOD to get that situation rectified. Now, that's not to say that GOD will force your husband to turn away from his adulterous ways and the marriage will work. That is to say that if you stay in GOD'S will, the will of GOD will be your portion; meaning, you will remain blessed. Some men repent, some don't, but what GOD will use you to do is to become a reflection of HIMSELF rather than reflecting your husband. A wife is a reflection of her husband, but when he steps outside the will of GOD, the wife has to take on the task of allowing herself to become GOD'S mirror. You do this by not getting in your flesh and not allowing your emotions to lead you into sin. In other words, it's okay to be angry, but you have to remember not to sin.

What Adultery Does to Women

As GOD reflects HIMSELF through you, what HE is doing is giving your husband an opportunity to repent and turn from his wicked ways. From there, your husband will either choose to repent of idolatry, thus enabling him to turn away from adultery, or he will leave you altogether. Now, I know there aren't many women who want to hear that their husbands may leave, especially women who know their husbands want no part of GOD, but the truth is, GOD has called you to peace. That man's adultery has put him at odds with GOD, and as such, he will become a tormented soul, even while still in the earth. Tormented souls are dangerous to themselves and others. For this reason, GOD gives us permission to divorce and remarry when adultery is a part of the equation. Trying to force an adulterous man to stay is not only dangerous for you, but it's dangerous for your children. Sure, it may seem difficult to fathom a life without the man you've come to love, but once you get over the initial shock of a breakup, you'll soon come to understand just how much GOD loves you. This is because you will get to see how

What Adultery Does to Women

GOD provides for abandoned wives who've chosen HIM over men. Eventually, if you so desire, GOD will send you a husband after HIS own heart, and you will look back and thank GOD you let go.

The Truth about the Mistress

There was a time when I was in the world and my mind was absolutely messed up. My thinking was nothing short of perverted, and during that time, I'd become like a city without walls. I didn't know how to control myself once those haunting, overwhelming sexual desires took over. Needless to say, I was not saved and definitely the home for many demonic spirits.

During this time, most of my friends were immoral and had no trouble sleeping with married men. Honestly, I didn't see too much wrong with adultery at that time. I had an "all's fair in love and war" mentality, and I thought the only men who strayed away from their wives were the ones whose wives were sexually neglecting them or emotionally abusing them. The whole concept of a man cheating on a good woman seemed too far-fetched to me. In my warped views, something

The Truth About the Mistress

had to be wrong with her. Nevertheless, I was never too fond of the idea of being some man's mistress, because I knew what being a mistress entailed, and that was sex with no commitment. In addition to not wanting to be some man's mistress, I knew I was extremely jealous, so I wouldn't make for a good mistress. For this reason, I avoided married men. Nevertheless, my inability to control myself landed me just where I didn't want to be, and that was in a sexual relationship with some woman's husband. Honestly, I didn't want a relationship with him, nor did I want to take him from his wife. I just wanted sex because I was a broken soul. I was single (in the natural anyway) and he happened to be near me when that urge came upon me. So, for a couple of months, we became bedroom buddies, but I ended the affair when I felt he was becoming too serious and too jealous. What does this tell you about the way I was? First off, I'm a woman and women should *never* be able to have sex with someone and not feel anything.

- I *was* broken.

The Truth About the Mistress

- I *was* demon-led.
- I *was* immoral.
- I *was* hell bound.
- I *would not* and *could not* be a good woman to any man at that time.

A mistress is an open grave. She has the equivalent of a soul tie with Satan, and any time a man joins himself to her, he joins a host of men who, through her, have become linked to the enemy through sex. She is a bridge between the soul of a man and Satan, and through her, many mighty men have been brought down.

Proverbs 6:26: For by means of a harlot a man is reduced to a piece of bread: and the adulteress will prey upon his precious life.

Proverbs 9:13-18: A foolish woman is clamorous: she is simple, and knoweth nothing. For she sitteth at the door of her house, on a seat in the high places of the city, To call passengers who go right on their ways: Whoso is simple, let him turn in hither: and as for him that wanteth understanding, she saith to him, Stolen waters are sweet, and bread eaten in secret is pleasant. But he knoweth not that the dead are there; and that her guests are in the depths of hell.

Believe it or not, a mistress is spiritual warfare manifested. She is the tool Satan uses to get men to rebelliously and blindly join themselves to him by joining themselves to her.

1 Corinthians 6:15: Know ye not that your bodies are the members of Christ? Shall I then take the members of Christ, and make them the members of an harlot? God forbid.

A mistress will speak many sweet-sounding words to a man, but this does not mean she is sweet, it simply means she's learned to hide her bitterness very well.

Adulteresses learn to prey on men by giving them whatever they say their wives aren't giving them, and this can include:
- Sex
- Perverted Sex
- Respect

The Truth About the Mistress

- The Ability to Feel Needed
- The Ability to Feel Wanted
- Someone to Relate to

Adulteresses don't just tailor to a man's lust, they pacify a man's needs, even when those needs are completely irrational. This is not done because she loves the guy and wants him for herself. Many times, a mistress is a broken soul who feels the need to compete with other women by sleeping with their husbands. When a man chooses to spend the night with his mistress, her confidence is boosted because his rebellious act toward his wife causes the mistress to believe she has a stronger pull on him than his wife. When a man leaves his wife for her, her joy is not in the fact that she has him all to herself; she relishes on the fact that she's won the tug-of-war between herself and that guy's wife. After that battle has been won, many mistresses have been known to abandon their newly single lovers when they "threatened" them with a committed relationship. Others choose to stay a little longer to ensure

The Truth About the Mistress

there is no reconciliation between the husband and his wife. Finally, there are those mistresses who will happily attempt to fill the wives' now empty shoes, only to find that they are either too big or too expensive for their sinfully clad feet.

There are different kinds of mistresses, but make no mistake about it, they are all soul tied up to multiple men (two at the least) and they are self-centered, even when they appear to be caring and regretful. Below are some of the mistress types I hung around when I was lost.

1. **The Brazen Mistress:** She's been hurt by many men and she doesn't care about hurting other women. After all, some guy she loved hurt her for another woman, so like a virus, she continues to spread the pain.
2. **The Silent Mistress:** She's quiet and shy, but don't take her silence to mean she's an angel. She's just craftier than the Brazen Mistress, and definitely more dangerous. She's also a skilled mistress; meaning,

The Truth About the Mistress

she's likely been involved with a few married men in her past.

3. **The Sensitive Mistress:** She keeps saying how bad she feels that she's sleeping with another woman's husband, yet, she continues to sleep with him. Truthfully, she may have a somewhat empathetic heart, but her selfishness outweighs her empathy, making her a man's worst nightmare.
4. **The Dreaming Mistress:** This woman has been living in her imaginations far more than she has been living in her reality. She has a plan for herself and she spends too much time imagining life the way she wants it to play out, but there's just one problem. She has no wisdom. She has not made plans for setbacks, delays, and cancellations; therefore, she is usually emotionally unstable and very opinionated. Life, for her, is a fairy tale in the making, but when reality hits her like a ton of bricks, she's usually the woman who falls the hardest and takes everyone tied to her

down with her.

5. **The Competitive Mistress:** She gets her self-worth from tearing others down. She wants to win, and she wants to win so badly, she will give the husband a chance to leave his wife, but if he does not do so in a timely manner, she will often resort to stalking, harassing, or leaving subtle clues for the wife. She simply wants to win. After she wins, she'll happily call the husband a loser before walking away from him.

6. **The Heroic Mistress:** She's always trying to rescue some woman's husband from a bad marriage. She easily becomes obsessed with every detail of her lover's marriage, and will often be found trying to get close to his family. This mistress has absolutely no problem attacking a man's wife. As a matter of fact, she's more likely to confront a woman she does not know than she is to walk past her if she were to see her, for example, at the park. But as brave and caring as she appears, her soul

is dark and her motives are impure. Any man who ends up in her bed has unknowingly renounced his soul.

7. **The Mating Mistress:** Her biological clock has been going off for a while, and she finds it difficult to get single men to settle down with her, so she goes after married men. She prefers married men because they've already committed to one woman; therefore, she believes they will have no problem committing to her. When this doesn't happen fast enough, or when she's grown tired of being used, she will often resort to trying to lock a man in. Her most effective weapon is her womb. She's the mistress who will flush her birth control down the toilet and swear it didn't work once she gets a positive pregnancy test. For her, it's not so much about winning the guy as it is about fulfilling her desire to have children or get a father for her already birthed children.

8. **The Contentious Mistress:** This rowdy

soul simply wants to fight. She's used to fighting women, and she's used to sleeping with men who are unavailable. She sleeps with them and immediately starts speaking reproachfully about their wives, even planning to confront or attack them, should she see them. It's not always about competition with her. She's simply broken, and we all know that hurt people hurt people.

9. **The Needy Mistress:** This lady needs her bills paid. She's had more eviction notices than she can count on one hand. She needs a man to help her with her bills, and she usually goes after men with decent-paying jobs or potential. In most cases, she's the one who's most adamant about a man leaving his wife because she absolutely needs help.

10. **The Gold-Digging Mistress:** She's similar to the Needy Mistress, but the difference is she wants more than her bills paid, she wants to live like royalty. This woman is

often seen wearing expensive designer clothes, driving a luxury car, and pulling into a well-to-do neighborhood. Unlike the Needy Mistress, any man who gets with her needs to have enough money to take care of her without his wife's knowledge; meaning, she typically goes after men with six-figure incomes. She's usually not interested in having some woman's husband full-time, she simply wants him to take care of her.

Of course, there are many categories of mistresses not mentioned, but they are all broken souls in need of deliverance.

Below are 20 truths most men (and some women) don't know about the adulteress.

1. **She's walking in unforgiveness.** Most "other women" have been hurt by someone, and all too often, their choices are a reflection of that pain.
2. **She's broken.** Not only is she walking in unforgiveness, but her soul is broken,

The Truth About the Mistress

causing her mind to be perverted. To be perverted means to be altered by an ungodly force to work against one's original design.

3. **She's not trusting or trustworthy.** Let's face it, she gets her guy by tearing down one of the holiest institutions in this earth: marriage. For this reason, she doesn't respect marriage or the vows said in marriage.

4. **She may pretend to be confident, but she's lacking in the self-esteem department.** Her pretentious nature is nothing more than concealer for her blemished soul. Most men don't realize how broken she is and how low her self-perception is until it's too late.

5. **She's a seductress.** To seduce means to lead astray. Her goal is to lead men astray....period.

6. **She's a tool used by the Delilah spirit.** Delilah seduced Samson with the intention of exposing him and his strength to his

enemies. An adulteress hunts for the precious soul of a man, and she does this by seducing him, and after he's been led astray, she exposes him to the enemy.

7. **Her soul is a grave for many lost souls.** Any time we have sex with a person, we join ourselves to that person in what is popularly known as a soul tie, but women are receptors, men are imparters. Any man who joins himself to her leaves a part of himself with her. This ungodly link to her serves as a bridge between her soul and his soul; thus, giving the enemy access to that man's marriage, sanity, finances, and his life.

8. **She's very crafty**, and will, therefore, listen to a man talk about everything he feels is wrong with his wife, and then, she'll pretend to be the perfect fit for him. She may even pretend to empathize with his wife on some things, but make no mistake about it, her motives are purely selfish.

9. **She takes great photos, but she doesn't**

make great movies. A photo is a frozen image, and anyone can smile in front of a camera for a few seconds. The flash of a camera is quick and people can go back to living their real lives outside of a camera's flash. But when you see her life in motion, she's not that happy-go-lucky woman she appeared to be on the photo.

10. **Her biggest fear is losing the man she's sleeping with to his own wife.** All too often, an adulteress will work overtime to ensure the man she's sleeping with does not reconcile with his wife. That's because she has some sort of competition going on in her mind, and to her, him going home to his wife means she has lost. She doesn't mind him leaving her for another woman, however, she just doesn't want him with his wife.

11. **She's usually entertaining multiple relationships at once**, but like most adulterous men, she has one guy who she prefers to be with over the rest, and he's

The Truth About the Mistress

usually the guy she can't have. It's not that she loves him the most or is more attracted to him than she is to her other suitors, a married man is more attractive because he's simply unavailable. If she were to "win" the married guy, she'd attempt to settle down with him, but she'd eventually get tired of entertaining her "consolation prize". After that, she'd likely go after someone else's husband, or she may retire her adulteress jersey and settle down with an available man.

12. **She's likely played the mistress before.** Now, she may pretend your guy (or whomever she's sleeping with) is the first married man she's actually entertained, but in most cases, this isn't true. If he is the first guy, he more than likely won't be the last because adultery is more than a choice, it's an ungodly heart condition.

13. **She is idolatrous.** Believe it or not, just as a cheating man worships himself, and therefore serves himself, a cheating woman

also worships and serves herself. Another woman's marriage, to her, is the perfect sacrificial offering.

14. **She may use religion or GOD as a cover**, but even a blind man can see she's not Godly. Many adulteresses deck the halls of their local churches with the intentions of pulling a "church guy" because they believe men in church will make better husbands. But to pull a Christian man, she has to learn to speak the Christian language, and she will likely learn to do this fluently. If she loved and feared the LORD, she would not be committing idolatry or adultery. Remember, you shall know them by their fruit (See Matthew 7:16).

15. **She has self-entitlement complex.** Many adulteresses are estranged from their entire families or many of their family members because of their ways; that is, unless their families are just like themselves. Because she doesn't have a solid or actual relationship with the LORD, she has not

allowed her flesh to die, and is, therefore, self-centered and entitled.

16. **She's offering lust, not love.** She doesn't know real love (GOD) from within the depths of her soul, and therefore, cannot truly love anyone else. Love has three depths it must reach before it's perfected in a man: The love of GOD, love for self, and love for others. When we truly love the LORD, everything else falls into place, but when our love isn't real, we give out imitations of love called lust, obsession, and dependency.

17. **She likes benefits, not responsibilities.** Many mistresses simply want to have fun, and the thrill of sleeping with another woman's husband may seem like the highlights of their lives. Nevertheless, many mistresses want the benefits and maybe even a title, but not the responsibilities. Believe it or not, many adulterous women want to wear the title of a wife, but want no part of the

The Truth About the Mistress

responsibilities of a wife. For this reason, many men who leave their wives and marry their mistresses find out the hard way that taking an adulteress to the altar is no different than trying to baptize a snake. Once it's dipped in holy water, it will still be a snake, only a wet snake. The same with an adulteress. Even once she's married, she will still remain an adulteress, only she'll be a married adulteress until she has truly repented of her sins, been delivered from every soul tie she's established in her sin, and has had her mind renewed. This process can take years, and in many cases, decades.

18. **She may be a professional mistress, but she'd make a horrible wife.** Again, I played the mistress and hung around many mistresses, so I can safely tell you that mistresses don't make good wives because they don't respect the sanctity of marriage. Most mistresses who end up as wives cheat on their husbands.

19. **GOD loves her.** Okay, so here's the part where a line is divided between the forgiving and the unforgiving. You see, GOD can't forgive you of your sins until you forgive others of their trespasses against you. This includes her. Always remember that she is a soul first and GOD loves her. Instead of lashing out against her (which she's used to, by the way), try praying for her and showing love and kindness toward her. I know that in your state of hurt, you may envision her and your philandering husband burning in the pits of hell while being forced to watch a movie of what they'd done to you for all eternity, but such thinking is wicked. GOD does not want your husband or his mistress(es) to burn in hell, HE wants them to repent. Remember this: We all deserve eternal damnation because of our sins against GOD, but since HE was forgiving enough to send HIS Son to die for our sins, we could at least extend that same forgiveness and love to others.

The Truth About the Mistress

After all, we don't have to die for their sins, we simply have to live with the reality of what they've done.

20. **She needs you.** Believe it or not, she's a victim; if not the victim of others, she's the victim of her mindset. As I mentioned in the previous point, she's used to people lashing out at her, she's used to living life on the defensive, so you lashing out at her won't help her at all. It only validates her thinking. Sometimes, the people who hurt us have one opportunity to see a demonstration of love (outside of GOD) and that opportunity may come through us. Sometimes, we just have to swallow our pride and tuck away our emotions to rescue another soul from eternal damnation. If you love, pray for (not against) and extend help to her when she needs it, you may be the soul GOD credits for winning her soul, and the favor of GOD will follow you all the days of your life.

Living with a Cheating Man

Living with an adulterous man is nothing short of agonizing. It's a test of one's faith, and it is really an experience that is so atrocious to GOD that it is one of the few reasons GOD permits us to divorce our spouses.

Living with an adulterous man is a challenge in itself because, on one hand, the wife sees the appearance of the man she's grown to love, but on the other hand, she witnesses a hideous creature moving about that she doesn't recognize. Trying to go about her normal life proves to be a daunting task because the man lying next to her every night is nowhere near normal anymore, nor is he familiar.

The hardest part of living with a cheating husband is a wife having to deal with her own hurts and not being offered any sort of relief from that pain; all

Living With a Cheating Man

the while, being expected to go about life as usual. The wife is expected to go to work with an unsound mind and be the best employee she can be, but this is next to impossible because her heart is broken and her mind is distracted by what's going on in her personal life. For example, I remember having a job that required its employees to be fully alert, and the employees were monitored daily at that company. To perform the job, I needed to be fully attentive, but my thoughts were all over the place. Again, one of my co-workers had told the entire office about Taylor's mistress calling her; plus, I was dealing with the agony of finding out he was indeed cheating. I ended up being written up repeatedly because of my performance until I finally broke down in one of the manager's offices. I was very ashamed because I'd been taught to keep my personal life private. My manager let me go home that day, and when Taylor found out that I'd broken down at work, he became enraged at me. I was emotionally unstable and at my wit's end. Less than two weeks later, I was in another manager's office having a meltdown. Such behavior was not in my character. I was just overwhelmed by what I was going through and I didn't know who to turn to or how to deal with it. That manager let me go home that day, and again, when Taylor found out, his response was insensitive and demeaning.

Sex is one spousal responsibility many adulterous husbands will not relinquish their wives from, and for a wife who knows, or suspects, her husband is cheating, sex can feel like strong-armed rape. Just as many kidnapped victims of rape willfully submit (out of fear) to their captors for the sake of surviving, many wives of adulterous men willfully submit (out of fear) to their husbands for the sake of maintaining the peace in their homes. Most women don't stay in bad marriages because they want to stay. In most cases, they want the dust to settle so they can be sure about their decision to stay or go. A wife who stays until she's sure she wants to leave is oftentimes a wife who will refuse to reconcile with her husband once she's left. A wife who leaves when she's angry is oftentimes a

Living With a Cheating Man

wife who will reconcile with her husband as soon as she calms down. For this reason, it is never wise to rush a woman into leaving her husband. It is always better to offer her love and support until she makes up her mind as to what she wants to do.

Most adulterous men don't want to leave their wives. They argue and fight with their wives because they want their wives to let them do what they want to do without complaining about it. They want to know that their wives will not leave them, and they want life to continue as normal. This mindset makes living with an adulterous man even more difficult because the wife will often try to reiterate to her husband that she cannot deal with his philandering ways, but the husband will try to reiterate to his wife that he's not going to stick around if she keeps accusing him of cheating. He knows she's aware of his infidelities, but he believes that admitting he's cheating may empower the wife; therefore, many husbands want their affairs to be a don't ask, don't tell event. So, the fighting evolves from being about a wife's suspicions that her husband is cheating to a husband's demands that his wife just stop looking for proof that the other woman exists. Of course, such thinking is cruel (and demonic) in itself, but until he's been delivered, a two-timing husband will see life through selfish eyes.

How can you continue to live with a man who's repeatedly breaking your heart? You change your mind about the situation and start looking at it from a different angle. You see, most women will yell at their husbands because they think that by doing so, their husbands will finally see their points and commit to a monogamous relationship. This type of thinking only sets the woman up for more pain. Instead, the best thing to do is take time to yourself and come to terms with the truth, and, from there, make an informed and Godly decision. Make sure GOD is involved in your decision and ask HIM to reveal the truth to you. If you know he's cheating, accept that he's cheating, and then, decide if you want to be married to a cheater. If you choose to stay, please understand that he will likely continue to cheat, so in staying, you are agreeing to the terms of the relationship he's now offering you. If you know you can't be with an adulterous man, pray about it, and if GOD gives you the clearance, walk away. As women, we often make the process a lot rougher because we choose to stay, all the while, trying to push our husbands to change. When we do this, it's because we think we can convince our husbands to be faithful. When life proves to us that we don't have the tools or the words to combat adultery, we find ourselves frustrated, argumentative, and desperate. You will eventually have to come to terms with what your husband is doing, and you will eventually be forced to make a decision, should he choose to keep doing it. It is better to embrace the truth now and start planning from there than it is to keep lying to yourself and have the truth to find you with no plan. Remember, you cannot change a man's mind, but you can change yours. Below are ten tips and recaps of what you should do if your spouse is committing adultery:

Living With a Cheating Man

1. Tell yourself the truth.
2. Accept the truth.
3. Decide what you want to do based on the truth you know.
4. Pray about your decision.
5. Get instructions from GOD before you move on your decision.
6. Stop arguing with the man. He is who and what he wants to be, and if GOD won't force him to change, neither should you.
7. If GOD tells you to leave, do it hastily. If GOD tells you to stay, pray for strength. If GOD tells you to stay still, don't move. If GOD tells you to move, don't stay still.
8. Don't tell your husband you're leaving if you get the green-light to leave. Just do it.
9. If you choose to stay, stop arguing about what he's doing. Just remain prayerful.
10. Don't resort to mental games and manipulation. I know that making your husband sleep on the couch and refusing to cook for him both sound like effective methods, but they aren't. Manipulation is

not the cure for adultery, the WORD of GOD is.

Another thing you should do (if you choose to stay temporarily or permanently) is to go out and do the things you love to do. Find your passion. Too much idle time will only give your mind opportunities to wander into some pretty dark places. Get to know yourself more, and find out who you are beyond what you've been through. For me, staying with Roger when I discovered his other woman was no picnic in the park, but truthfully, I stayed because I wanted instructions from GOD as to what to do. I turned to many people in leadership and received various opinions, but I knew if I left, I'd only be doing it to retaliate. I wanted to leave when GOD said I could leave. I had no idea what GOD was planning to do. All I had were assumptions, and again, I thought HE was going to clean the man up and make him a better husband. Instead, GOD used that time to build me up, give me a greater confidence and faith in HIM, teach me my value,

Living With a Cheating Man

and ripen me with wisdom. Before I knew it, I was a different woman married to the same man and I found my focus shifting from Roger and his lies to the assignments and gifts GOD had given me. I found peace in HIS will. I found joy in HIS will, and I was able to peacefully cohabitate with a man who loved himself and his family more than he loved me. I wasn't so offended with his ways anymore, because I eventually came to realize that the marriage would end someday and there were a few lessons in that marriage that GOD wanted me to get. As to not delay my (or his) departure, I sought out those lessons diligently.

Your peace is in the will of GOD, but you have to come outside of your flesh to retrieve it. You have to come outside of your understanding to live in it, and you have to come outside of your religiousness to keep it. Yes, living with an adulterous man can be agonizing, but if you marry GOD'S plans for your life, the LORD will have you floating around your house, in love with HIM and enjoying your life. While you're busy living a blessed life, the LORD HIMSELF will deal with your husband. Let the LORD court your mind, and HE will rebuild you in such a way that no man will be able to tear you down again. HE did it for me in the midst of a horrible marriage, and my situation was extreme; therefore, I know HE will do it for you.

Should You Leave or Stay?

I remember wishing GOD would just give me a plain answer. Just tell me to leave or give me the strength to stay. I didn't want a series of signs or puzzle pieces I had to put together myself, I simply wanted the answer spelled out in a way I couldn't question or doubt. And I worried. Had HE given me the green light to leave and I'd missed it? Did HE want me to stay in that marriage? Was staying in that marriage my punishment for not having waited on HIM? After having done things my way all of my life, I was *absolutely* determined to hear from HIM before walking out of that marriage, but I worried maybe HE'D spoken and I'd ignored HIM. I thought I'd missed my flight outta there, so I remained prayerful that GOD would grant me another chance to be set free. Nevertheless, I knew there was wisdom, knowledge, and understanding in that marriage that GOD wanted me to take out of it, so I started asking for the

Should You Leave or Stay?

lessons. I didn't want bits and pieces of the lesson. I wanted to get the whole lesson so I could hurry up and get out of there, or GOD could hurry up and change the man I'd chosen for myself....*whichever plan HE had.* I didn't care either way. I just wanted to escape my manifested reality.

Most women ask themselves and others whether they should leave or stay. Most Christian women turn to GOD for answers, and like myself, they begin to wonder if they've missed GOD when those answers don't come fast enough. Should you leave or should you stay? The answer is as simple as it is complicated. It's not up to you or me, it's up to GOD, and GOD makes the final cut based on your husband's heart.

Can you leave an adulterous man? Of course you can. Should you stay with an adulterous man? The answer lies within yourself. Can you deal with what he's doing? Can you get used to the idea of sharing your spouse with someone else? Can you

Should You Leave or Stay?

find peace in a home knowing that your husband likely has two homes? If you can and you want to stay, then stay. But if you know you can't deal with his infidelities, pray about it, and if GOD gives you the open door to leave, walk right out of it. You see, when GOD gives you permission to leave, HE will always give you somewhere to go. It might not be where you want to be, but it's definitely where you need to be for a season.

One thing I've come to understand is that some women can stay with adulterous men, and even though it may hurt them to know what their husbands are doing, they stay with those men despite how they feel. And guess what? Neither you nor I can judge them. The world calls them weak because the world doesn't understand the difference between weakness and strength. It takes a *lot* of strength to stay with an adulterous man. The easiest thing to do is walk away, as hurtful as walking away may be. It's not wrong for you to stay, just as it isn't wrong for others to go. Every woman has her own measure of faith and

Should You Leave or Stay?

strength, and we should never criticize another woman just because she's not as strong as us, she's too strong for us, or we don't understand her strength. For this reason, I always tell the loved ones of adultery victims to let them get tired for themselves. We can get tired for them, but we're not the ones who can decide for them. Until they are tired and until they've had enough, they will continue in those marriages.

Whether you leave or stay is between GOD and yourself, but remember, GOD has called you to peace. With that being said, whichever direction you find peace in is the direction you ought to be heading.

1 Corinthians 7:15: But if the unbelieving depart, let him depart. A brother or a sister is not under bondage in such cases: but God hath called us to peace.

1 Corinthians 14:33: For God is not the author of confusion, but of peace, as in all churches of the saints.

Matthew 10:13: And if the house be worthy, let

Should You Leave or Stay?

your peace come upon it: but if it be not worthy, let your peace return to you.

Psalm 34:14: Depart from evil, and do good; seek peace, and pursue it.

When You're Not Ready to Leave

You've planned to get out of that marriage plenty of times, only to find yourself feeling overwhelmed at the thought of leaving. Now, your husband is so used to you threatening to leave, his confidence has graduated to cockiness. His words have become crueler and the atmosphere has become thicker; nevertheless, you're just not ready to leave.

Your loved ones are upset with you for staying, and you're somewhat upset with yourself for not being able to just walk away. But just like clockwork, your husband does something hurtful, and you've made up your mind (once again) that today's the day you're going to leave him. The next day comes and you're still there, and you begin to resent yourself for it. The pressure from your family to leave, the weight of the world's judgments, and your own resentment for yourself is making your life miserable. Nevertheless, you feel compelled to do something. Often, when a wife begins to feel anxious, it's because of the following:

- **Pride:** Pride tells us we're stupid for staying. Pride questions our self-respect and causes us to resent ourselves. We also begin to resent our spouses for making us resent ourselves.
- **Religious Uncertainty:** Religious uncertainty is usually the result of misinterpreting the scriptures or religious leadership.
- **Familiar Pressures:** Familiar pressures include the pressures placed on wives from their friends and family members. All too often, women stay with their adulterous husbands because they want to know that the decision to leave was their own decision, but constant familial pressures make them question whether they really want to leave their husbands or if they're feeling compelled to do so because of their

loved ones' persistent interference.

- **Unforgiveness:** When your spouse is hurting you, it's pretty easy to fall into unforgiveness, and once resentment sets in, it's difficult to stay with the person you resent.
- **A Bothersome Mistress:** Some mistresses are so determined to "win", they start harassing their lovers' wives. Some are brazen and will openly taunt their lover's wives, while others are cunning and will subtly harass their competitors. When I was married to Taylor, he had several mistresses. One was subtle, and the rest were brazen. The subtle one kept quiet and didn't harass me until Taylor told her he was ending their relationship to work things out with me. (Subtle mistresses are usually skilled at playing the mistress and they've learned that being brazen usually gets them the opposite of what they want). One of the more brazen women took it upon herself to go through the phone book and call every

When You're Not Ready to Leave

Buckner (my maiden name) who lived in my city until she reached my mother's house. Once she called my mother's house, she told my brother to send the message to me that she was sleeping with my husband. Of course, her problem was that she couldn't get him to leave me, so she tried to get me to leave him.

- **Worrying About Her Children:** Most mothers do not want their children to see them down, and therefore, motherhood makes the pressure a little more intense because the mother wants to return to her normal state of mind for the sake of her children. She knows that if she stays with her adulterous beau, she may never retrieve her sanity. Because of this, many mothers become anxious to leave when they realize their pain is beginning to affect their children.

When you're not ready to leave, you're just not ready. The hardest part is getting over how you

When You're Not Ready to Leave

feel about not leaving. You can't allow external pressures to determine what you do, just as you can't allow all of your negative emotions to drive you to make a permanent decision based on temporary feelings.

Below are a few tips and suggestions for you, if you're not ready or sure you want to leave your husband:

1. **If your husband isn't physically abusing or threatening you, don't tell everyone about your situation.** Sometimes, it's better to just share what's going on with your pastor and no one else. The reason is, you get so many people emotionally involved in your relationship to the point where they begin to pressure you to do what they feel you should do. This changes their perception and attitude toward your husband, and should you decide to stay, you may end up losing relationships with the people you've shared your story with.

2. **Don't keep threatening to leave your husband.** He heard you the first six

hundred times. When you're ready to leave, you'll leave...*if that's what GOD tells you to do, of course.* Repeatedly threatening to leave someone could desensitize them toward your words or cause them to react violently. Instead, only convey to your spouse how you feel about his adulteries, and make it clear that you want him to stop. If he doesn't stop and you decide to leave, just go.

3. **If you decide to leave, don't advertise it.** Sometimes, women get so emotionally charged up, they start taunting their husbands with their decisions to walk away. This can prove to be dangerous. Always remember that some men are cruel enough to cheat, and they're also cruel enough to kill a woman who won't accept their infidelities. The safest way to leave is when he is at work and you have family and friends with you who will help you pack. I heard a guy once say that his sister had decided to leave her husband while the

husband was at work. She'd asked her brother to come over to help her pack. While he (the brother) was in another room of the house packing, the husband returned and started beating the wife because he didn't realize her brother was there. When the brother heard the commotion, he immediately ran to his sister's rescue and beat her husband until he broke away and fled for his life. Had she not taken the wise route, her husband could have really hurt her, or worse than that, killed her.

4. **Don't pack and unpack your clothes.** *Okay, so I was guilty of this crime....repeatedly.* I kept telling myself I was going to leave, but once my clothes were packed, I realized I didn't have anywhere I wanted to go. Sometimes, the problem was I just wasn't ready to go. Again, packing your clothes can prove to be dangerous.

5. **Stop arguing with your husband about his infidelities.** Speak softly and lovingly,

and just let GOD do the rest. Yelling at him won't change his mind. It'll only give him the green light to respond to you negatively, and sometimes, a man who's emotionally vacated his marriage can be pretty cruel.

6. **Don't ask your husband questions you don't really want the answers to.** Sometimes we ask questions out of curiosity when we are in no ways ready for the response.

7. **Don't harass the mistress or respond to her harassment.** Harassing or responding to the mistress only gives her the power to hurt you more. I decided to taunt one of Taylor's mistresses when she'd called my house to harass me, but that conversation ended up with her describing my bedroom in full detail to me. Needless to say, I hung up feeling sick.

8. **Don't be retaliative toward your husband.** I know how hard it is to continue living as if nothing happened, but remember this: if you want GOD to move on your

When You're Not Ready to Leave

behalf, you have to be still. If you refuse to
be still, GOD won't move!

The most important thing to remember is to just keep living. I know it's hard to do, but GOD has already made plans for your situation, and the only cooperation HE needs from you is that you sit down so HE can stand up. The sooner you obey HIM (consistently), the quicker HE will deliver you from that situation. Maybe your marriage will work out. Maybe your husband will repent and turn his life around. But whatever happens is what's going to happen anyway. By obeying GOD, you are simply refusing to delay HIS response.

When you're not ready to leave, don't overwhelm yourself with negative thoughts about yourself. Don't be burdened down by unforgiveness and don't give the enemy any opportunity to live or vacation in your heart. Instead, continue to cook, clean, and do all the things you ordinarily would do. This doesn't make you stupid and it doesn't mean you are without a plan. It simply means you

When You're Not Ready to Leave

plan to let GOD deal with it.

In the Meantime

Personally, I think the hardest part of enduring an adulterous spouse is the uncertainty of what tomorrow (or today) will bring. Will the marriage work and the two of you go on to use your experiences to help others? Or will it end and the two of you go your separate ways? Not knowing which direction your life is going in is like driving down a busy freeway while wearing a blindfold. It's scary, emotionally draining, and it's definitely a time that is as painful as it is humbling. And because it's a scary time, as women, we often try to speed up the process by questioning our spouses, threatening to leave them, conducting our own investigations, and begging GOD for the revelations we feel we need. Nevertheless, those answers can never seem to come soon enough.

So, what should you do while you are waiting on GOD for direction? Should you continue to run yourself mad by trying to find the answers yourself? Or should you just leave? The answer is simple, seek peace and pursue it. Wherever your peace is, that's where you need to go, *and, of course, I don't mean you should run into the arms of another man.* If you can find peace in your own house, stay there until GOD gives you further instructions. If the environment in your home is too thick with negativity, go to a place where you can find peace and GOD, of course. Never go from one bad environment to another unless the environment you're in is dangerous for yourself or your children, or you believe yourself to be a danger to the people in that environment.

Waiting to get instructions from GOD or to see which direction your marriage is headed in can be an excruciating process, but it's often made harder by the victim's unwillingness to step outside of the victim mentality and step into the mentality of an overcomer. How you see yourself will determine how you treat yourself.

When Taylor and I broke up, I initially saw myself

In the Meantime

as a victim. Because I saw myself in the wrong way, I looked for others to rescue me; thus, the reason I ended up with Roger. Because of how I saw myself, I ended up losing my home, my car, and almost everything I had. I was too busy seeing myself as a victim, I didn't realize that every title we step into, we come in as a rookie, but as time goes on, we ascend the ranks of that title. Therefore, people who see themselves as victims start off as rookie victims, and if they're not delivered from that mindset, they end up becoming professional victims. Thankfully, GOD dealt with me and I decided to grab onto HIS unchanging hand so I could be changed. When Roger and I broke up, I didn't see myself as a victim, I saw myself as a woman who'd just been set free from a very bad situation. I recognized GOD throughout the process and I knew HE had just delivered me from a bad marriage. I recognized the fact that GOD was giving me another chance at life, and I knew if I wanted to be blessed to have a peaceful and joyful life, I'd better take my second chance seriously.

In the Meantime

Before Roger and I broke up, I didn't sit around the house waiting to see what would happen. Instead, GOD blessed me to learn many skills and start many businesses. Instead of wasting my time yelling at Roger about his choices, I spent most of my days and nights building onto my business, filling customer orders, or learning something new. By the time that marriage ended, I'd written many books, having taken the lessons I was learning in that marriage and published those lessons for others to learn from. I'd become so distracted with work, writing, and learning new things, many clues of Roger's infidelities went unnoticed, and that's not a bad thing. I didn't need to focus on what he was doing; after all, those things would've driven me to the brinks of insanity. Instead, my focus was on GOD and every assignment HE had given me. I was determined to please HIM and become a better woman. I watched myself grow into a woman who was not only blessed, but a woman I didn't recognize. I was (and am) so proud of the woman I'd become, I continued to multiply my talents by obeying GOD. You see, I'd made up my

In the Meantime

mind that I wasn't going to sit around and feel sorry for myself. Instead, I would just build. I would build the ministry GOD gave me. I would build the businesses GOD gave me. I would write the books GOD put in me. I would help the people GOD assigned to me. In other words, I decided to not allow pain to make me self-centered. I decided to not even entertain pain; instead, I handed Roger over to GOD and I went about my FATHER'S business. Before long, Roger's antics didn't hurt as much anymore. I stopped running myself mad by trying to check his cell phone and I stopped trying to see what he was up to next. More than that, I stopped allowing myself to feel like I was a fool for staying with him. I stopped being his victim, and when I did, he lost power over me and I found success in my LORD. What's amazing is...even when Roger left, I was too busy to care. Now, that's not to say that the pain didn't eventually hit me, because it did, but it is to say that the impact was lessened by my unwillingness to enter the emotions the enemy wanted me to enter. I cried, but I praised GOD for delivering me.

In the Meantime

I acknowledged to GOD that I understood some of what HE was doing and I was okay with it, and whatever I didn't understand at that time, I knew HE'D give me the understanding later on (if HE saw fit). I'd get over the pain of going through another divorce, but I could never get over the pain of being married to the wrong man for the rest of my life; therefore, being set free Roger (and his sister) was bittersweet.

The point is: GOD has a plan for you, but you may not understand what it is right now. Don't focus on everything your husband is doing, because if you do, you'll spend your days and nights in pure misery. Follow the instructions that are clear to you right now, and let the other instructions come as they may. If GOD told you to start a business, get up and start that business. If GOD told you to go back to school, go ahead and start registering for school. Anything GOD tells you to do is preparation for the path HE has created for you and is vital to your healing. Who knows if your marriage will work or not? Nevertheless, whatever

In the Meantime

GOD decides to do with your union will be made easier if you will only obey HIM now. I am glad I obeyed GOD because, in doing so, I was blessed to be able to keep my residence, buy a car (because Roger took the only car we had), and live better than I did when Roger was around. I was blessed to be able to enjoy life without worrying about how I would pay my bills, and I did all of this with no college degree. I learned graphic design through the direction of the HOLY SPIRIT. I wrote books, established businesses, and taught classes without any formal training. Instead, I leaned and depended on GOD, and HE proved HIMSELF to be JEHOVAH JIREH, my provider.

While you wait for GOD to instruct you, get busy in purpose and learn to enjoy your life in the midst of a storm. Don't see yourself as a victim; that mentality will only ensnare you and cause you to want revenge. See yourself as an overcomer, and by doing so, you will see and believe that something good is going to come out of your situation.

Romans 8:37: Nay, in all these things we are more than conquerors through him that loved us.

1 Corinthians 15:57: But thanks be to God, which giveth us the victory through our Lord Jesus Christ.

Matthew 24:10-13: And then shall many be offended, and shall betray one another, and shall hate one another. And many false prophets shall rise, and shall deceive many. And because iniquity shall abound, the love of many shall wax cold. But he that shall endure unto the end, the same shall be saved. And this gospel of the kingdom shall be preached in all the world for a witness unto all nations; and then shall the end come.

To the Loved Ones of the Victim

I understand that it hurts you tremendously to see your loved one in pain, and you want to reach out, remove her from that situation, beat her husband into an unrecognizable pulp, and repent on Sunday morning; nevertheless, at this moment, all she needs is your love and support. Coming against her husband will not work in your favor because she's still undecided, and this puts her in a position where she feels she's being forced to choose between you and her husband. This is absolutely too much weight to put on an already broken soul.

When I was married to Taylor, I kept his affairs and abusive behavior a much guarded secret from my mother. The only person who knew was my closest friend, and I'd told her because she was going through the same thing with her husband, and I knew she wouldn't judge me. I wanted to tell

To the Loved Ones of the Victim

my mother, but I knew that doing so would only upset her and make her feel like she needed to get involved. I knew she'd try to drag me out of that marriage kicking and screaming, and I didn't want to feel pressured to leave when I wasn't sure what I wanted to do just yet. As a matter of fact, at that particular time, I was still wrestling with whether I believed Taylor's lies or the voice from within. But once I started having breakdowns at work and the pain started feeling almost unbearable, I finally decided to confide in my mother. She'd come by my house one day, and we'd sat around chatting about life in general. When she'd gotten up to leave, I walked her outside, and while on the porch, I finally said those words she was dreading to hear. Not only was the man I married to cheating on me, he had been physically attacking me. As suspected, my mom was livid and she immediately started telling me to come back home; nevertheless, as crazy as it sounds, I just wasn't ready to return to her place. I was still confused about what I wanted to do, and I still had some shred of hope in me that Taylor

To the Loved Ones of the Victim

would change.

After sharing my story with my mother, I immediately felt a sense of relief, but I also began to feel humiliated. After all, I'd always been a strong and confident woman. How in the world had the once feisty and ever-so-confident me fallen into such a low place? The worst feeling of them all, however, was knowing she was expecting me to leave, but not being able to follow through. So, for a while, after sharing my struggles with her, I kept quiet because I didn't want to worry her. I would try to make her think our marriage had become better. It goes without saying, I could not hide the truth from her, because she could hear the pain in my voice. Eventually, she stopped pressuring me to leave and started telling me that whenever I was ready to leave, her house was open for me.

Sometimes, pressuring a person to leave only confuses them and may even cause them to stay longer than they ordinarily would have stayed.

To the Loved Ones of the Victim

The reason is, we often want to feel like our decisions to leave are our own. We want to know we walked away because we wanted to walk away, as opposed to wondering if we'd walked away because we'd been told to walk away.

The best thing you can offer a victim of adultery is your love and support, and sometimes, a listening ear. Offering to have someone beat up (or beat down) your loved one's husband is not a good idea. *I'm glad my mom finally grasped that reality.* Below are 11 things you can do to help your loved one find their way.

1. **Compliment her often.** Believe it or not, she is likely starved of compliments, so your complimenting her will help to build up what her husband has torn down.
2. **Tell her daily, and as often as you can, that you love her.** All too often, victims of adultery feel unloved, and these feelings can lead them into some pretty dark places.
3. **Offer a listening ear, but don't become a doormat.** Please understand that there is

To the Loved Ones of the Victim

a difference between helping someone versus letting someone dump on you. How do you know the difference? If your loved one has made it clear that she has no intention of leaving her husband, yet, she complains about him, she's using you to relieve herself. In such cases, it is better to request that she not talk to you about her home life. If your loved one expresses that she is not sure if she wants to leave or says that she is definitely planning to leave, be that listening ear she needs to help her make a decision. Sometimes, it's not your advice that will steer her, it's hearing herself telling you what she's going through that will help her to see herself from an objective viewpoint.

4. **Help boost her self-esteem.** You can do this by setting her up for a glamour photo session, taking her out to a nice restaurant, or just with a few words.

5. **Encourage her to further her career or get into her purpose and support her**

To the Loved Ones of the Victim

with everything in you. Here's an amazing fact: A woman who's able to sustain herself financially is more likely to leave an adulterous husband than a woman who's dependent on him. Never give her money to leave, or she may disappoint you by spending it on her husband; instead, encourage her to be as great as she's designed to be.

6. **Encourage her growth in the LORD.** If she's young in the faith, she's not going to have enough faith to walk away or make a good decision in regard to her marriage. Read the Bible to her and with her, take her to church with you, and encourage her to get closer to GOD. The closer she gets to GOD, the more the voids in her life will be sealed up, and the less power her husband will have over her. Why do you think some men go out of their way to insist their wives not go to church? They fear their wives will be made whole again, empowered, and suddenly realize they don't need them.

To the Loved Ones of the Victim

7. **Provide plenty of comic relief for her.** In a house riddled with adultery, there isn't much laughter. The atmosphere is thick and negative, so she can definitely use a few laughs. Always provide a better atmosphere and some comic relief, even if you have to take her to a local comedy show.

8. **Respect her wishes.** There will be many times that you'll feel you have the answers to all of her problems, and you may feel passionate about sharing and enacting those answers, but always remember to respect what she wants. If you don't, she will not turn to you for help anymore; instead, she may find herself turning to people who don't have her best interests in mind. Just keep saying these words to her: *Whatever you want to do, sweetie.* Such kind and merciful words make it easier for her to deal with the issues in her marriage with a clear mind.

9. **Encourage her independence.** One of

To the Loved Ones of the Victim

the things GOD did with me when I was married to Roger was teach me how to be alone. HE started encouraging me to go places alone, knowing HE was with me. Before long, I'd begun to love my time spent alone with the LORD.

10. **Encourage her to help others.** You'd be absolutely amazed at the healing power of helping others. *Seriously.* As I mentioned earlier, GOD handed my purpose to me and started using me to help others while in the midst of a bad situation, and healing was almost instantaneous! If she's the victim of abuse or adultery, simply take her down to a shelter for abused women, and the two of you should do some volunteer work there. After helping so many women and hearing their stories, she will likely begin to feel compelled to help herself.

11. **Talk to everyone in your home and encourage them to be loving and supportive, not judgmental.** Sometimes, victims won't return to their parents' houses

To the Loved Ones of the Victim

because of contentious, judgmental, or prying relatives. In my case, I didn't want to return to my mother's house (either time) because I feared I was going from one bad place to another because my siblings were still at her house and we'd always had pretty contentious relationships.

To the Husband of the Victim

Before I speak to you, I want to say this: I get nothing out of speaking with you about your marriage. I'm not trying to passive-aggressively rebuke another man because I am happily divorced and living a worry-free life. I was married twice, and I went through fragments of hell in both marriages, but I've forgiven the men from my past because they did what they knew how to do. At one point in my life, I was broken too, and I hurt people; therefore, I can understand that my exes were simply in moments of darkness. I tell you this because I don't want you to think I'm getting something out of this when I'm not. I simply want to help.

At the same time, I know you're likely saying that you can be "nagged" by your wife. You don't need to hear another woman rambling on and on about the dangers of adulterous affairs; nevertheless, I respectfully ask you to read this chapter, at least.

To the Husband of the Victim

You've probably glanced over this book, and if you've read even a portion of my testimony, you've likely told yourself that you're nowhere near as cruel as the men I'd married. You're likely looking at all the things you provide for your wife and all you've done for her, so in your mind, a quick (or extended) lay-cation with your mistress is fully justifiable. (Such thinking is very common for men entangled in adultery). After all, you've made up your mind that you're not going to leave your wife for your mistress, you're just having a little fun. Your mistress is more than likely more outgoing in the bedroom than your wife is, and there's a reason for this. In the marketplace, we called this competitive ad-matching. Ad-matching is what many retailers do to stay competitive. For example, if I were to see an ad displaying a bicycle on sale for $79 with one retailer, I could easily take the ad to that retailer's competitor. The competitor will either match the price or give me a slightly lower price just to get my business. Mistresses do this, too. You can be entertaining a sexually lazy woman, and she may start off as

To the Husband of the Victim

vibrant, energetic, and without limits in the bedroom, simply because she's being competitive. Later on, she'd reveal her true bedroom personality, and likely blame her laziness on some handicap. If your wife exits the picture, and the mistress realizes she has you to herself full time, she'll stop pretending.

I definitely won't be hard on you, so please don't be on the defensive. My goal is to restore your marriage, if that's what you want. If not, my purpose is to help your wife to transition into her new reality, and that is a reality minus your presence. One of the reasons I'm addressing you is because when I was married, there were many, many times I wished someone would step up and speak on my behalf. You see, I'd said everything I knew how to say, and I'd said it over and over again until the men I'd married learned to tune me out.

I understand. You plan to do what you want to do until you're tired of doing it, and you want her to

To the Husband of the Victim

stop complaining and just accept it. I know. Again, I was married twice and suffered through adultery both times, and I *have* to tell you that adultery is crueler than death itself. Adultery deals a repeated blow to a woman's heart.

You're probably telling yourself that she deserves it. After all, she yelled at you, refused to sleep with you, talked with her ex-boyfriend, stayed out too late, stayed mad at you for too long, or whatever it is that she's done that makes you feel justified in your actions. But let's be honest here. Your decision to sleep with another woman has absolutely nothing to do with your wife. Adultery has everything to do with selfishness, greed, and lust. Adultery is the symptom of idolatry; meaning, you turned away from GOD first, and this resistance trickled on down into your home. Now, some mistress is offering you what you feel you aren't getting at home, something you feel you're entitled to, and to you, the affair feels like a harmless rendezvous, but it's not.

Adultery hurts far worse than you know or could

To the Husband of the Victim

even remotely imagine. If GOD has given us permission to divorce one another because of adultery, you have to know that it's no small issue. Nevertheless, you've made up your mind as to what you want to do, but before you lock it in as your new reality, let me share a few facts with you:

1. **Forty percent of first marriages end in divorce.** Fifty percent of second marriages end in divorce, and sixty percent of third marriages end in divorce. This means your chances of staying married are greater with the wife you have.
2. **GOD made you the head of your home.** How you run it, run it down or run from it reflects on your leadership. Make GOD proud and take control of yourself before you end up being consumed by greed.
3. **Mistresses are immoral...period.** I played the mistress once, I hung around a bunch of adulteresses, and I have to be honest with you. There's no such thing as a moral mistress, regardless of how nice she pretends to be.

To the Husband of the Victim

4. **Selfish women don't make for good wives.** An adulteress is unsympathetically selfish and this is obvious in her willingness to tear down another woman's marriage for her own selfish gain.
5. **Most men who leave or lose their wives for their mistresses end up realizing how great their wives were**, but in most cases, when this happens, it's far too late.
6. **Your mistress is not a blessing; she was sent to attack and destroy your marriage and lead you astray.** If you fall for it, not only will you lose the favor (wife) GOD has blessed you with, but you will also expose your children to a life of growing up without you. Take charge over your mind before it's too late.
7. **An adulteress is an open tomb, designed to bury naïve men alive.** Every time you lie with her, you are ripping away parts of your soul and leaving it with her, and that's why you have trouble cleaving to your wife. The enemy is using the other

To the Husband of the Victim

woman to divide you.

8. **Women are strong, but don't test your wife's strength.** You've probably noticed your wife's strength and decided she can take it, but adultery breaks down even the strongest of women. Adultery is a manifestation of idolatry, and idolatry has hurt and upset GOD so much, HE has allowed nations to be taken into captivity and destroyed because of it. Adultery is the equivalent (in human potency) of idolatry, and it hurts far more than you can ever imagine. You're supposed to be the strong one. You're supposed to love and protect your wife. If she acts strong, it's because she's had to be strong. Take that strength upon yourself so she can be soft again.

9. **It's not too late, regardless of what has happened.** If your wife is still there, it's because she loves you and is trying to make it work. Tell her the truth, but first, talk to the LORD and repent for idolatry. Give your wife the ample time to heal and

To the Husband of the Victim

commit to GOD, yourself, and your wife to never do it again.

10. **Whatever your mistress is giving you, you can get it from your wife...unless it's perverted**; meaning, it's against GOD. Either way, you need to seek deliverance from idolatry and adultery, and once those two fall away from you, sexual perversion will fall away from you.

11. **Remember, marriage is working with your wife, not against her.** Just as she's not perfect, the other woman isn't perfect either. One of the most important lessons I learned while playing the adulteress (I was going through a divorce when I met Roger, so I was an adulteress) was that we often see our spouses' faults and think they are deal-breakers. The outside person doesn't have those same faults in particular, so we think we're getting a better deal with less stress. When I met Roger, I was going through a divorce from Taylor. Taylor had two main issues I absolutely could not live

To the Husband of the Victim

with, and they were: (1). He didn't quite grasp the fact that a man was not supposed to physically attack a woman, and (2). His appetite for other women. Nothing could be worse than an abusive cheater, right? That's what I thought until I ended up with Roger. Roger wasn't physically abusive, but he was definitely a cheater. Roger didn't cheat with multiple women (that I know of). There were two who I was absolutely confident he'd cheated on me for, and a few possibles. Roger was in submission to his sister, and she was not only unsaved, she was demonically controlling and bitter. I'd never really seen her smile, except a few times when she had been drinking. Mara hated my guts because I wouldn't submit to her; after all, Roger was in submission to her. Even though we lived states away from Mara, she called Roger every day to make sure her strong arm of control was not weakening, and Roger was so afraid of her,

To the Husband of the Victim

I had literally seen him tremble when she'd become upset with him. Roger looked like a better deal until I bought the lie.

12. **I hung around many mistresses in my darkest hours, and I once played the mistress, so I am confident I can spill a few truths on your lap.** You probably won't be receptive of these truths now, but later on, you'd definitely revisit them and nod your head in affirmation. Your mistress has two or more personalities. She has her real personality, which is likely the one you haven't met yet, and she has her custom-fit-for-you personality. The custom fit personality is an advertisement designed to give her the edge over your wife. She may agree with your wife on a few things, because she doesn't want to be too obvious, but for the most part, you're not sleeping with "her" per-se. You are sleeping with the decoy of what you want, a decoy that's nothing more than bait on the end of Satan's fishing line. Nevertheless,

To the Husband of the Victim

once she reels you in, you'll discover how dark her heart is. Know this, the adulteress is not a great listener, she's just learning what you want (for now).

13. **David repented after he slept with Bathsheba and had her husband killed, but his actions set off a string of events that haunted him for the rest of his life.** There was the death of his first child with Bathsheba; his son, Amnon, raped his daughter, Tamar; his son, Absalom, killed Amnon to retaliate for Tamar's rape; his son, Amnon, tried to kill him to take the kingdom from him; his son, Amnon, ended up getting his head caught in a tree and dying, and his son, Solomon, (in his old age) started intermarrying with pagan kingdoms and his wives turned his heart from GOD. The point is, one mistake can set off a domino effect that will haunt you for the rest of your life. There's no sex worth dying for, nor is there any woman worth destroying your family for.

To the Husband of the Victim

14. **Sarah gave Hagar (her handmaiden) to her husband, Abraham, to marry, but this act was against GOD.** GOD told Abraham (Abram at that time) that he would be the father of many nations, and Sarah (Sarai at that time) was old and doubted GOD because of her age. In those days, it was not uncommon for men to have several wives, but only one wife was recognized as the official, GOD-approved wife, and she was the first wife. Any other woman was considered a concubine, meaning, she was a wife *only* through sex. Sarah gave him permission to sleep with Hagar because of her unbelief. But when Sarah told Abraham to kick Hagar and her son, Ishmael, out, Abraham didn't want to, but GOD told him to "hearken" (which means listen) to the voice of his wife. The point is, to keep the blessings, sometimes you just need to keep the peace. It was silly for Sarah to send Abraham to sleep with her handmaiden, but it was wise for Abraham to listen to GOD on

To the Husband of the Victim

behalf of his wife. Had he ignored GOD, he would've probably kept Hagar and lost Sarah, or the peace in that home would've been lost forever. One of the worst things you can do is send peace out of your home.

I know that sharing those facts and many other facts with you may or may not change your mind about the lifestyle you've chosen for yourself, but at least, you will have the luxury of making an informed decision. Your wife doesn't know me personally (more than likely) and I don't know her personally; therefore, I stand to gain nothing by sharing these truths with you. I only want you to take a moment and consider the direction you're heading in, and not the direction the enemy told you that you were going in, because he is a liar. He'll show you white picket fences, beautiful vacations, unlimited passion, and everything you want...all wrapped up in an adulteress, and that's because he's like a cheesy car salesman. His goal is to dress a lie up and sell it to you. If you buy it, you give him full rights to yourself and the

To the Husband of the Victim

relationship you've established on his foundation (lies, lust, betrayal, deceit, manipulation). Some of the greatest men around have been with their wives and stuck with them through thick and thin for decades. Once GOD saw HE could trust those men with HIS daughters, HE knew HE could trust them with health, wealth, a sound mind, and all the blessings HE likes to drench HIS children with. But the ones who could not be trusted were often found in miserable places, pretending to be happy.

My recommendation (your favorite part because men don't like many words, they love solutions) is that you:

1. **End the relationship with the mistress.** Okay, so you told your wife there was no mistress and you're in too deep right now to just pull out, but it is better to end it now than to let it end your marriage.
2. **Tell your wife the truth.** If you don't tell her, I can almost guarantee you the mistress will. It will be easier for her to hear it from you than it would be for her to hear it

To the Husband of the Victim

from someone else. When Taylor finally admitted to his adulteries, I felt a huge sense of relief on top of the pain I'd been dealing with. The relief was because I finally saw an end to his two-timing in sight and I realized I wasn't losing my mind.

3. **Repent to GOD for your idolatry.** Your first sin was self-worship.
4. **Repent to your wife for your adultery.** Be 100% honest with her, holding nothing back except the lurid details.
5. **Restore order in your home** by creating a schedule for you and your wife to talk about what happened and what needs to happen. This way, you don't have to worry about random conversations that leave you feeling uncomfortable. For the first week, set up one hour a day to talk about the affair and what led up to it. After that, set up thirty minutes for discussions every three days. Do this for a month. After a month, set up one hour in each week for any questions that need to be answered,

To the Husband of the Victim

and do this for two weeks. After that, don't discuss it anymore. Agree to put it behind you and always remember to comfort your wife when she's hurting because of it. You can't dictate how long she gets to hurt. That pain will stay around for a long time, and that's why I recommend setting up those talks and letting her speak to you, question you, and allowing yourself to be truthful and transparent with her. Of course, you don't have to talk as much as I mentioned; it's up to you as a family. You'll find that when you're open to talk, the wife won't talk as much.

6. **Bind pride.** One of the nastiest spirits that get into a man when he's double-dutching between women is pride, and that spirit is not only haughty and cocky, it's downright nasty. Humble yourself and do not give in to those lies you hear that sound like:

•She's just trying to use the situation to control you.

•She likes drama and that's why she's

To the Husband of the Victim

trying to keep it up.
•You know she can cry at the drop of a hat.
Please know this: she is your wife and you need to protect and love her, not break her. GOD entrusted you with her, now make HIM happy HE did.

7. **Go to Christian counseling, if necessary.** Don't be prideful and refuse this option at the expense of your marriage.
8. **Love never fails, but people do.** Don't fail your wife and children.
9. **Going through a midlife crisis? Get a motorcycle**, not a mistress.
10. **GOD loves you and HE will forgive you if you repent.** All the same, your wife may be hurt and upset, but she may forgive you as well. Just love her past this and never take her (or GOD) through it again.

Transitioning into Your New Reality

I truly hope your marriage works out, your husband repents, and the two of you find peace again in the arms of the LORD. Nevertheless, the sad and inevitable truth is, so many marriages won't make it past adultery. Adultery is a spirit that attempts to block a couple's journey together toward the blessings of GOD. Sadly enough, many men and women are seduced by the spirits sent out to draw a wedge between them and their spouses. The enemy's plan is to encourage selfishness in a man, and from there, he causes him to pity himself. Once he begins to pity himself, the enemy will then send a woman into his life who will offer her (false) condolences, while priming him for the enemy. Remember, the enemy comes to steal, kill, and destroy. He comes to devour, and a mistress is the seasoning he uses to prepare a man for consumption.

Transitioning Into Your New Reality

But for anyone whose marriages doesn't work, please know that GOD has a plan for you that's far greater than the plans you've had for yourself. HE will bless you with the life you want and the spouse you need; a spouse who can make it past the spirit of adultery by binding it, and he will go on to collect more favor from GOD with you. Nevertheless, in the meantime, you shouldn't be thinking ahead, you should be thinking about today.

Honestly, when Taylor and I first broke up, I had no clue what I was going to do. I had no plans for my future, nor did I have any idea how I was going to pay all of the mounting bills, but somehow, I knew everything was going to be okay. I knew I just needed to take things one day at a time and try to adjust to my new reality. My biggest struggle was being alone without enough wisdom to sustain me, so I ended up in another relationship rather quickly.

When Roger and I broke up, I had the wisdom,

Transitioning Into Your New Reality

knowledge, and understanding I needed to remain single until GOD sent the appointed husband for me. I'd learned to enjoy my life as a single woman, and I no longer saw singleness as a guest who overstayed its welcome. I began to love being by myself, all the while, enjoying the new confidence I had in CHRIST. You see, I knew that I'd never sin against GOD again to get a mate, so I knew I wouldn't end up marrying another ex-husband-to-be. I knew the appointed one was coming and I smiled, thinking about the time we'd spend together. I laughed, thinking about all of the "while you were away" stories we'd someday share with one another. But, in the meantime, I knew what I had to do, and that was that I had to live. I simply needed to live each day as if it were my last, and to love on the LORD each day more than I did the day before.

I can't pretend that I was completely happy seeing Roger go. On one hand, I was elated because I'd asked the LORD to either change Roger or remove him from my life. Losing Roger meant I

Transitioning Into Your New Reality

didn't have to deal with his condescending views of women or his overly-controlling and intrusive sister anymore. On the other hand, losing him meant I had to start all over again and get used to a life without him, so again, the end of our marriage was definitely bittersweet.

I noticed that GOD begins the transitioning process with us while we are still married because HE knows when a marriage is going to end. HE sees the depth of pride and sin his adulterous and estranged sons are in, and HE knows how much those men will have to go through to get them to humble themselves and repent. All the same, HE knows who's willing to repent and who's not willing to repent; therefore, once a man begins to reject GOD repeatedly, HE begins to prepare HIS daughter (that man's wife) for the inevitable: a divorce.

You are your husband's favor, so in losing you, he loses his favor from GOD. Sure, things may be looking up for him right now, but more than likely,

Transitioning Into Your New Reality

you're the reason he's been blessed by GOD. You're the reason his career is climbing, his finances are stable, and he has a glow about him that draws man's favor to him. He doesn't realize this because he's become accustomed to living in favor, and therefore, does not associate it with you. The enemy won't tell him that by losing you, he's about to lose everything. Instead, the enemy is showing him a painting of a city that doesn't exist and promising to make him king of that city.

What about you? How can you adjust to your new reality if the marriage ends in divorce or separation? Below are a few tips and suggestions that should help you.

1. **Your husband didn't build you, so he shouldn't be able to break you.** The enemy loves to mess with a hurting woman because her heart is broken and exposed. It's easy for him to get bitterness into a heart when it's exposed. At the same time, the Bible tells us that GOD is near the brokenhearted. Don't lean toward hatred,

lean on GOD. Remember, be angry, but do not sin.

2. **It's your life. You can choose if you are going to be happy or not.** Life is but a series of decisions, and you have the power to decide whether you choose to be happy or not. No one can decide for you if you're going to let your pain consume you or let GOD heal you. Your husband's mistress doesn't have that power to ruin you (unless you give it to her), your husband doesn't have that power (unless you give it to him), and Satan doesn't have that power (unless you turn it over to him). Decide against all odds and against your pain that you will be happy. Know this: it's all about attitude. When Taylor and I broke up, I decided I'd be okay and I ended up okay. When Roger and I broke up, I decided my life would be great and it has been awesome.

3. **Forgive your husband and his mistress or mistresses.** One thing I always tell

grieving women is to go ahead and ask the LORD to put forgiveness in them while they are still grieving. The reason is: grieving is a lengthy process for most women, and it's better to be healed, restored, and delivered all at once than it is to be healed at one time, restored at another time, and delivered after the restoration process is finished. I prayed that prayer after Taylor and I broke up, and GOD stepped in and placed so much love in my heart for Taylor and the mistress he'd left to be with, that I questioned whether it was real or not. I felt a peculiar love and sense of compassion for them, and it was completely genuine. I did the same thing with Roger and the love GOD gave me for him transitioned from a romantic love to a brotherly love. I began to pray for the salvation of his soul because GOD loves him and so do I. Sure, both men were bad to me in so many ways, but they treated GOD far worse than they treated me, and if HE can forgive them, so

Transitioning Into Your New Reality

can I.

4. **Live your dreams. Learn something new.** There is so much to you that you don't know just yet. Now is the time to unearth your talents and live your dreams. Learn something new. Learn how to cook more dishes, or learn how to cook...period. Learn a new language, visit some countries you've never visited before, or start a new company. One of the biggest setbacks women face is letting go of their plans with their exes and figuring out what they want to do as individuals. All too often, the plans we have aren't plans we would have ordinarily come up with had we been single. Many times, our plans are the plans we've made with our spouses. Before Roger left, GOD blessed me to start a business, and by the time he'd left, I was making enough money from that company to live comfortably. And get this, I didn't go to school to learn any of the things I was doing; they were simply talents I'd buried

Transitioning Into Your New Reality

years ago. I also went out and got the dog I'd been begging to have for so many years. I started living life to the fullest, and I enjoyed (and continue to enjoy) every new blessing GOD sent my way. I had to sort out what dreams were mine and what dreams were "ours" so I wouldn't waste time pursuing "our" dreams. For me, separating my plans from "our" plans was like separating his things from my things so we could move on.

5. **Don't rush into any new relationships.** One of the greatest snares placed before grieving women is the men who are all-too-willing to rescue them. You have to know that GOD wants to heal, deliver, and restore you before HE sends your appointed husband to you. You have to be delivered from the soul ties you've established in your life, you have to sort your plans from your ex's plans, you need to fully grieve, you need to forgive the ex, and you need to be restored and renewed

before even considering a whole new relationship. All the same, learn from your failed marriage. Don't just go out and pick your own guy because you'll only pick him according to your right-now needs and voids, but later on, he may not be a good fit for you. This time, let GOD choose your spouse. Don't rush it, just live.

6. **Don't enter any new friendships unless GOD leads you into them.** Like many broken women, after Taylor and I broke up, I opened myself up to new friends and that was just not the right thing to do. You have to understand, I was still in a broken state; therefore, most of the women who I opened my heart and home up to were also broken. It's not uncommon for us to go out there and let our emotions lead us into friendships we end up having to pray our way out of. Some women can hang around you when you're broken, but if they ever see healing on your horizon, they'll try to chase it away with gossip, criticism, or

painful reminders of your past, or they'll run for cover. Again, be led by the SPIRIT of GOD, not by your emotions.

7. **Don't try to rush your healing, only try to perfect it.** We want to heal and we want to heal fast. Our understanding often tells us that if we want to move on, we need to start over, so we try to start over as fast as we can. Moving on isn't about getting into a new relationship or holding back your feelings, it's about letting your heart completely heal. After Taylor, I tried to rush my healing with people and they ended up being the very thing that ensnared me and set me up for Roger. After Roger, I knew not to rush my healing but to take it one day at a time, but I did try to drown out my actual feelings by claiming the feelings I wanted to have. Of course, this didn't work and I had to take the time out and face how I really felt, as opposed to trying to fast forward my healing. Needless to say, I soon discovered why rushing one's healing

isn't a good idea. Every day and every tear is not only vital to your healing, but it's a chapter in your life that's designed to keep you from traveling down that same path with a different person. All the same, it's a setup for a clear and realistic testimony, one that will help many women to heal and understand that their extended pain isn't abnormal, it's a normal part of the healing process.

8. **Don't focus on your ex, focus on your GOD.** Any time I counsel women, I find that the large majority of them are still focusing on their exes and the lives of their exes. They know who their exes are dating (or married to) and many of them even know where the guys live. A lot of times, women tell me they've learned this information from their "best friends", not understanding that their besties are being used by the enemy to hold them back. I don't check on my exes because their business is none of my business. We've had lives and plans

together, but now that we live apart from one another, we have to think apart. The point is, you will get so much further if you'll only focus on today, and the people in your life today, rather than focusing on yesterday and the people who were a part of your yesterday. Honestly, I believe a lot of women have unknowingly and repeatedly rejected the blessings of GOD because they were too focused on the men in their pasts. Let go and move on in the LORD.

9. **Cast down evil imaginations and every high thing that exalts itself against the knowledge of GOD.** It's late at night and you're just watching a little television before turning in. The movie goes off, and all of a sudden, a memory surfaces. You remember some bad thing your ex did to you, and with that new memory comes a new revelation. Now, you're ready to mentally delve back into those memories to try to see what else you may have missed. This is a common trick of the enemy. The

battleground he likes to fight you on is your mind, and for this reason, you have to take the Sword of Truth, which is the WORD of GOD, and pierce every imagination with it. You should never allow yourself to be entertained by flashbacks; instead, focus on the day you're in. Additionally, the enemy will try to weigh you down with lies. He loves to taunt, ridicule, and expose women to the evils of their flesh. Make sure your thoughts are fresh, not rotten, meaning, they are new and not old. Old memories are nothing more than reminders of what GOD has brought you from, but new plans are thoughts of what GOD can bring you to. Never entertain thoughts of your past, unforgiveness, or any negative emotion.

10. **Your life didn't end, it's only just beginning.** Having the wrong attitude about the breakup can set the tone for the rest of your life and every relationship you enter thereafter. The best revenge you can

Transitioning Into Your New Reality

have on a man who's done you wrong is no revenge at all. Just keep on living and being blessed. Love like you've never been hurt and live like you've always been loved...because you have. GOD said HE will never leave nor forsake you. Don't focus on the people who left you, focus on the GOD who's stayed by your side throughout it all.

The Right Response to Adultery

When a husband commits adultery, it's not uncommon for the wife to become emotional and unstable. After all, she didn't just love her husband, she trusted him, and she centered her future around him and his words. All the same, she gave him her most treasured possessions: her body and her trust. The wife not only has to deal with the betrayal, but she also has to come to grips with the harsh reality that she's invested the best of herself into an unstable relationship. That's similar to putting every dime you have (if you were a billionaire) into a stock market, only to watch that market crash. Everything she has built, planned, and dreamed up is now wrapped up in her marriage, and her husband's adulteries has threatened every ounce of security she has. For this reason, it is not uncommon for an emotionally traumatized wife to make some pretty bad choices in her darkest hour. As I mentioned earlier, with

The Right Response to Adultery

Taylor, I allowed my pain to drive me into the arms (and bed) of another man, only to regret that decision. I'd also seen this behavior with many of the women I'd known over the course of my life. One of the most common responses to an adulterous affair is another adulterous affair.

Understand that every action that takes place in the realm of the earth inspires a reaction. You will always respond to what someone has said or done to you, even if that response is not verbal. For example, if a mistress attempted to bully one man's wife, the wife may respond by physically attacking the mistress. If that same mistress were to bully another man's wife, she may respond by calling the police. Another wife, on the other hand, may respond by ignoring the mistress, but more than likely, she will respond to the mistress's behavior by talking to her husband about it. In other words, no good or bad deed ever goes unanswered. Of course, GOD wants us to give those problems to HIM, and the way we do this is not by remaining unresponsive (which is pretty

The Right Response to Adultery

much impossible). We do this by responding in a Godly way. We pray about it, refrain from retaliation, and we have to forgive everyone who has offended us. Nevertheless, the emotional trauma that a wife endures during or after her husband's adulteries can be painful enough to cause the wife to respond with violence. For this reason, we have to fill ourselves with the WORD of GOD to the point that when we are stretched and broken by the trials of life, the only thing that will fall out of us is the WORD of GOD.

There is a right and a wrong way to respond to an adulterous affair, but we will always respond based on the abundance of our hearts. You see, when we're pressed, whatever is found within our hearts will begin to seep or pour out of us...even if those ways were mentalities we'd picked up because of our pain. That's why I ended up in an adulterous affair when I was married to Taylor. Adultery was still in my heart because fornication was still in my heart, and this became evident after Taylor and I split up. My response to Taylor's

The Right Response to Adultery

affairs was to have an affair of my own. If Taylor hadn't committed adultery against me, I surely wouldn't have committed adultery against him, but adultery would have been a sin that lied dormant in my heart. We all have to understand that it isn't the acts we involve ourselves in that's the problem, it's our wicked hearts. If Taylor had been a faithful man and treated me well, I could have ending up standing before GOD on Judgment Day and heard HIM refer to me as an adulterer. Of course, such a term would've been confusing to me if I'd never committed adultery against Taylor, but if the will to commit the act of adultery is within our hearts, we are adulterers; that is, until we've been changed by the renewing of our minds. The point is, whatever you are will come out whenever you're pressed.

The right way to respond to an adulterous husband is to pray for him, and to let him know (or remind him of) the following:
- His choices are hurting you.
- His choices are hurting, or will hurt, your

The Right Response to Adultery

kids.
- Adultery is a sin.
- You won't stick around if he continues or is involved in an adulterous affair.

Another thing you should do is give yourself and your husband a timeline. For example, tell your husband that he has one week to end his adulterous affair or face the consequences. Of course, most adulterous men won't respond well to ultimatums, but at least they can't completely act dumbfounded should you carry out your threats. It goes without saying that you should use wisdom when giving threats and ultimatums as some men can be dangerous.

After having confronted your husband about his adulteries, it is always better to remain silent and be watchful than it is to constantly talk to him about his choices. He needs time to think about what he's doing and to reconsider the consequences of his actions, and if you keep yelling and crying, you may overwhelm him. You want him to make a logical decision, not an

The Right Response to Adultery

emotional one. If he ends the affair because he doesn't want to hear you yelling or crying anymore, he's likely going to return to that affair once things calm down at home. After all, he didn't end the affair because he wanted to end the affair, he ended it because you wanted him to end it. On the other hand, if he ends the affair logically, it will have been because he took the time out to think about what he was risking to engage in that affair. Your silence will not only serve as an opportunity for him to hear himself think, and maybe even hear from GOD, but your silence will put the necessary pressure on him to make a swift and permanent decision. This means that if he chooses to end the affair, it will be because he weighed the pros and cons and decided it just wasn't worth the risk. If he chooses to continue the affair, it's only because he doesn't believe that you'll carry out with your ultimatum or he just doesn't care if you leave or not. In this case, it is better to depart from such a man and let GOD heal your heart rather than sticking around and trying to change that man's mind.

The Right Response to Adultery

Always remember that you will respond based on what you've allowed to enter your heart. With that being said, the WORD of GOD tells us to be angry, but sin not. It's okay to be angry with your husband, but it's not okay to sin against GOD because of what your husband has done. Everything may be speaking to you (your husband's affairs, his mistress, your finances, your health, your emotional stability), but it's how you answer that will determine what response GOD will give you. If you want the right answer, respond the righteous way.

Common Scriptural Misinterpretations

When I was married to Taylor, I'd come to realize our marriage would likely end in divorce, and that revelation was scary to me. I had a relationship with GOD, but I wasn't an avid Bible reader back then, so there was a lot I didn't know. I'd just began to accept that Taylor had a different vision for marriage than I did, and I started trying to pull my heart out of the marriage before it finished crumbling. I didn't want to feel the full impact of a broken heart, and I was scared to face an unknown future. Truthfully, my relationship with Taylor was idolatrous. I didn't realize it at that time, but I loved him more than I loved GOD. *I'm almost ashamed to say that, but I've learned better now.*

When I realized Taylor wasn't going to stop cheating, I started trying to make sure we could legally divorce in GOD'S eyes and I could remarry.

Common Scriptural Misinterpretations

I wanted to be married more than anything, but I'd come to believe that a wife could never divorce her husband; therefore, she could not remarry. Of course, I based those beliefs on my misinterpretation of 1 Corinthians 7:10-11, which reads, *"And unto the married I command, yet not I, but the Lord, Let not the wife depart from her husband: But and if she depart, let her remain unmarried, or be reconciled to her husband: and let not the husband put away his wife."*
I'd also read the scripture that states if the unbeliever wants to depart, let him depart; nevertheless, I was confident Taylor didn't want to leave me. I knew he was just being sexually greedy, he wanted multiple women, and his staying out for days at a time was his extended temper tantrum. He wanted to teach me a lesson, using my own heart as a weapon against me, and I'd finally surrendered to the reality that our marriage was doomed. Being a wife who turned a blind eye to her husband's infidelities was just not a role I was willing to accept, so I searched the scriptures for a way out.

Common Scriptural Misinterpretations

During that time, one of my closest friends was going through the same thing. Her husband had left her for his mistress and she wanted to make sure she could remarry after they divorced. We read the Bible to each other from time to time and discussed our findings. There had to be a way out. We both believed there was no way GOD would force us to stay married to the men we were married to. We turned to others who were avid Bible readers for answers, and had received many interpretations and misinterpretations of 1 Corinthians 7:10-11; nevertheless, regardless of what they said, the end of those marriages were inevitable.

The day after I received irrefutable confirmation that Taylor had been staying with one of his mistresses, I filed for divorce. I still wasn't sure what GOD'S plans for me were, but I knew I needed to get out of that marriage while I still had my sanity. I continued to search the scriptures and pray for understanding, and GOD answered. Below, you will find common religious

Common Scriptural Misinterpretations

misconceptions or questions, followed by the truth. As with anything, I encourage you to pray about what I've said. I've already prayed about it, but you need to hear GOD for yourself, especially in this hour.

Scripture: 1 Corinthians 7:10-11: And unto the married I command, yet not I, but the Lord, Let not the wife depart from her husband: But and if she depart, let her remain unmarried, or be reconciled to her husband: and let not the husband put away his wife.

Misinterpretation: If a wife divorces her husband, she has to remain unmarried for the rest of her life.

Verdict: This isn't applied to every case.
When the Bible told us (wives) not to "depart from" our husbands, GOD was telling us not to "leave" our husbands. In the biblical days, women could not file for divorce, only men could. But some women would leave their husbands and go back home to their parents. You'll notice that the scripture tells women not to "depart from" their

Common Scriptural Misinterpretations

husbands, but it goes on to tell husbands not to "put away" their wives. The term "put away" in the biblical sense means "to divorce". GOD was telling wives that they should not leave their husbands (You know how we do when we get mad and want to teach them a lesson). HE was also saying that if we left, we were to remain unmarried, or in other words, untouched; meaning, we should not join ourselves to any other men. The Bible goes on to tell us that we can be reconciled to our "husbands". I highlighted the word "husbands" to show you that the author is acknowledging that the woman he's speaking to is still some man's wife, and she could reconcile to him, but she was not to join herself to another man. In other words, if you have a temper tantrum and move back into your parent's house, you have to remain pure and untouched because you are still married.

Scripture: Romans 7:1-4: Know ye not, brethren, (for I speak to them that know the law) how that the law hath dominion over a man as long as he

Common Scriptural Misinterpretations

liveth? For the woman which hath an husband is bound by the law to her husband so long as he liveth; but if the husband be dead, she is loosed from the law of her husband. So then if, while her husband liveth, she be married to another man, she shall be called an adulteress: but if her husband be dead, she is free from that law; so that she is no adulteress, though she be married to another man.

Wherefore, my brethren, ye also are become dead to the law by the body of Christ; that ye should be married to another, even to him who is raised from the dead, that we should bring forth fruit unto God.

Misinterpretation: If a divorced woman remarries and her husband is still alive, she is an adulteress.

Verdict: If you read the entire scripture above, you'll notice the author (Apostle Paul) is speaking to those who are under the law, which we know to be the Old Testament law. He said that he is speaking to those who "know" the law; meaning, they are "one with" or in submission to the law. He also mentioned how the law has dominion over a man for the rest of his life. Finally, he goes on to

Common Scriptural Misinterpretations

say that his brethren (those of whom he was speaking with) are dead to the law through the body of CHRIST.

Scripture: Luke 16:18: Whosoever putteth away his wife, and marrieth another, committeth adultery: and whosoever marrieth her that is put away from her husband committeth adultery.

Misinterpretation: Anyone who divorces and remarries is an adulterer.

Verdict: This isn't always true. If you notice, the scripture says that a man who divorces his wife *and* marries another woman commits adultery; meaning, he put away his wife for the sake of marrying someone else. In the biblical days, many men had multiple wives, but they knew not to divorce one to be with another one; they simply took another wife. But their wives of old remained with them and were provided for by them. Of course, adultery is a sin, so we know not to engage in it, but truthfully, the majority of men who commit adultery have no intention or desire to leave their wives. They simply want to entertain

Common Scriptural Misinterpretations

multiple women, and with our culture, such thinking is not only taboo, but it's grounds for divorce. The second part of Luke 16:18 states that anyone who marries a woman who has been "put away" or divorced commits adultery. Please understand the depth of that scripture. We aren't married because of vows. Our vows are just our declarations to GOD that we will conduct ourselves according to the law or the WORD (whichever we are in submission to), but it's sex that joins two people. Therefore, we take a vow before GOD that we will uphold the law or the WORD in relation to the person we intend to lie down with *before* we become one with them through sex. With that being said, if you've ever had sex with another man, you are married to that man; that is, until GOD divorces you from him. This means that the average believing woman wasn't single before she married whomever she legally married. In other words, both parties committed adultery, albeit, unknowingly. The verdict is, if a man stops "sleeping with" a woman and another man comes behind him and sleeps

Common Scriptural Misinterpretations

with that woman (days, months, years, or decades later), both he and that woman have committed adultery. Nevertheless, we can be freed from both legal and illegal marriages, should we repent to GOD, meaning, we turn away from the sin itself and turn back to GOD.

In man's court of law, a divorce can take anywhere from 31 days to a year, but with GOD, the severing of soul ties can often take years (sometimes less) because of the depths of those soul ties. It's not because it's too much work for GOD, because it isn't. It's often because GOD provides the renewed mindsets we'll need, but we have to embrace them. HE opens the doors we need to receive our deliverance, but we have to go through them. Once we embrace new mindsets and go through those doors, we often find there are still new things we need to learn and more doors we have to go through, and this process makes the soul weary. So, a woman who has become one with a man through sex is married, and therefore, if she joins herself to another man,

Common Scriptural Misinterpretations

she has committed adultery. If a woman has repented of her sins, meaning, she has turned away from those sins and back to GOD, she is no longer guilty of the transgression since repentance is casting our burdens upon the LORD. CHRIST bore our sins in HIS body, so in repenting, she takes on the righteousness of CHRIST, and casts her burdens upon HIM, and, of course, we know, those burdens have already been dealt with by the blood of the Lamb.

Scripture: Matthew 5:31-32: It hath been said, Whosoever shall put away his wife, let him give her a writing of divorcement: But I say unto you, That whosoever shall put away his wife, saving for the cause of fornication, causeth her to commit adultery: and whosoever shall marry her that is divorced committeth adultery.
Misinterpretation: The Bible favors men.
Verdict: The Bible does not favor man, it favors righteousness. But GOD steps in to protect women when their heads (husbands) begin to emotionally or physically abuse them. That's

Common Scriptural Misinterpretations

because men are stronger than women, but GOD is stronger than man. Additionally, up until now, many people read (or shall I say, misread) the Bible in a way that made it seem as if it favored men while binding women, and that's not true. A wife is her husband's favor, and is therefore, favored by the LORD. Read Matthew 5:31-32 again. You'll notice the author is saying that anyone who divorces his wife, except for the cause of fornication, causes "her" to commit adultery. For years, that scripture has been translated to mean that the only way the man could leave his wife was if "she" fornicated. I actually had that understanding, too, for a while. The scripture is actually showing who's to blame for her adulteries. If the husband divorces her and she has not cheated on him, he, being the husband, has led his wife into adultery. This means that not only is she in sin, but also her husband, being the head of his home, has lead her into sin, meaning, he has her blood on his hands. If she commits adultery against her husband, on the other hand, she is responsible for

Common Scriptural Misinterpretations

her own adulteries, and her husband will not shoulder any of that blame. He is then free to divorce her and remarry, and he won't be held accountable for her actions.

What does this mean for you? The same guidelines that GOD gave to men govern women, meaning, if your husband commits adultery against you, you can legally divorce him and be free to remarry, but remember, you have to be led by GOD so you don't end up in adultery. You will be one with your current husband until GOD says otherwise. So, you need to be open to hear from the HOLY SPIRIT so HE can remove you from that union, but if you do things on your own, you may endanger yourself or miss out on what GOD wanted you to have.

Example: One week before Roger and I broke up, I'd began to feel overwhelmed and anxious to get out of that marriage. I'd already gone to the local Wal-Mart and purchased some moving boxes and tape a month or so prior, because things seemed to be growing worse and felt almost unbearable in our marriage. There had been many times that I'd wanted to leave him, and each time, the LORD had me to stay. Again, I worried I was missing GOD, or maybe, I was misreading His signs, so there were days I considered doing things in my own strength. But a week before he left, I found myself feeling emotionally bankrupt and overwhelmed, so I pulled my boxes out and started packing. Roger sat in the living room and ignored me as I packed my clothes, and even his ignoring me bothered me because I'd begun to question whether he had even a minute speck of love for me. The atmosphere was so thick and tense, I decided to get out of it and go looking for another apartment. I put on some clothes, grabbed the car keys, and headed out the door. It was a Sunday, so I knew I wouldn't be able to go into any apartments to view them, but I just wanted to feel like I was making a move toward getting out of that situation. Sitting still made me feel trapped and anxious.

While driving around through the parking lots of some nearby apartments, I decided to pray. After

Common Scriptural Misinterpretations

all, I'd learned to consult with GOD before making any major moves, and I knew I was upset and I didn't want my emotions to cause me to disobey GOD. As I was praying, the LORD kept telling me to go back home. I couldn't fathom going back to our apartment, but I knew to trust GOD. I knew HE had a plan, so after riding through a few parking lots, I decided to go back home, reminding myself I could go online to search. I wasn't sure what GOD wanted me to do, but I was sure the marriage was broken beyond repair....*for me, at least.*

A week later, Roger voluntarily and immediately moved out and we immediately started trying to initiate divorce proceedings.

When Roger moved out, I told him he could take anything he wanted out of the house, but he didn't want anything. He'd already taken his clothes and computer the day he'd moved, so I ended up keeping the apartment we'd lived in, the furniture (even though I got rid of most of it), and the electronics. I didn't end up with the burden of

Common Scriptural Misinterpretations

trying to relocate in a state where I had no family or friends. GOD had a greater plan for me than I did for myself. I wanted to move, but GOD removed Roger. Had I done what I wanted to do, the blessings probably wouldn't have followed me, but because I got over myself and obeyed GOD, the blessings stayed right with me. The point is, let GOD move you, and don't be moved by your emotions. When you let HIM do it, HE will provide a way of escape for you, and HE will not let you fall. Obeying GOD didn't just ensure that I'd have some place to stay, but obeying GOD ensured I would be free from Roger (soul ties and all).

Scripture: 1 Corinthians 7:15: But if the unbelieving depart, let him depart. A brother or a sister is not under bondage in such cases: but God hath called us to peace.

Misinterpretation: A wife (or husband) should work at their marriages, even when their unbelieving spouses want to leave.

Verdict: There's a reason GOD said to "let" the unbelieving spouse depart, meaning, do not try to

Common Scriptural Misinterpretations

hinder or stop them from leaving. Whenever you follow the WORD of GOD in relation to your spouse, what GOD is using you to do is to reflect HIMSELF through you. In obeying HIM, you allow yourself to cast a reflection of HIS love, mercy, and forgiveness time and time again. During this time, HE begins to tug at your husband's heart, but not so much as it relates to you, but HE deals with your husband about his relationship with HIMSELF. The reason is because when a man turns from GOD, he turns from the instructions GOD has set in place for him, and these instructions include how he should treat his wife. Nevertheless, even though the LORD will use you to reflect HIMSELF through, HE still does not infringe upon that man's will. Instead, HE gives him a choice. Repent and turn away from his sins, or walk away. If the unbelieving spouse chooses to walk away, it's not you who he is rejecting, he is rejecting the GOD who is reflecting through you. Your love, forgiveness, and compassion reminds him of everything that's wrong with himself, and because you are not being prideful or vengeful, he

Common Scriptural Misinterpretations

finds himself having to bear the blame and this can be overwhelming for him. After all, he can't put that blame on you because you are reflecting love and forgiveness. During this time, a man who wants no part of GOD will find himself feeling depleted because he's no longer battling a war against you, he's battling against GOD by coming against you. Feeling drained and defeated, he will likely pack his clothing and leave.

James 4:7: Submit yourselves therefore to God. Resist the devil, and he will flee from you.

There are many scriptures that are commonly misquoted in relation to marriage and divorce, but it is always important for you to ask GOD for understanding for yourself rather than accepting someone else's understanding. There are many leaders who will lead you in different directions, using different scriptures if you were to confide in them, and that's because some people minister from unresolved issues (unforgiveness), some people minister in accordance with the WORD of GOD, and some people tell others what they want to hear. The answer to your prayers will always

Common Scriptural Misinterpretations

manifest itself to you, but you just have to know when GOD is speaking versus when HE'S not speaking. Additionally, don't take HIS silence to mean HE'S upset with you and ignoring you. In many cases, HE is watching over you and letting the seasons pass because HE has a designated time that HE has called you to be restored. Don't move prematurely, and don't stay with your spouse because of fear. If GOD tells you to get out, be obedient and do it quickly.

Surviving an Affair Together

Let's get one thing straight, an adulterous affair isn't something you get over, it's something you have to get past. To get over it means that you're expected to shake it off as if it didn't happen. To get past it is to acknowledge that it did happen, but put it behind you as you continue your lives together. Many marriages have survived adultery and been restored through CHRIST JESUS. In our generation, most women are expected to leave their husbands after it is discovered that their husbands have been unfaithful; nevertheless, many wives choose to stay and work on their marriages rather than abandon them. Adultery can destroy a marriage, but GOD can raise that union up again and cause it to be stronger than before. Of course, both parties must be repentant and willing to put away their selfish idols and focus on loving one another yet again. First and foremost, GOD has to be restored as the head of that marriage so the husband can properly lead and cover his wife, and the wife can learn to respect and submit to her husband.

Believe it or not, adultery is an attack against the institution of marriage. It is nothing short of demonic, and the spirits behind adultery (lust, envy, wrath, greed, anti-Christ) all have one agenda: to sabotage marriages by causing the husband and wife to operate as two instead of one. As two, they are powerless against the enemy because they are out of order with GOD. As one, they are powerful against the enemy because they are bound together by the WORD of GOD, and are therefore, too powerful for the enemy to divide. That's why it is very important for a couple to operate as a united front and find ways to get past their individual feelings rather than being divided by offense. The hardest thing for a couple to do is to cleave to one another and see one another as a part of themselves because we tend to focus on our differences. Any time one of the parties in a marriage starts focusing on him or herself, that marriage begins to split down the middle. When couples begin to divide from within their own homes, feelings start getting hurt and rather than trying to heal as a unit, the individuals in that union may seek to heal individually. Of course, when the enemy can convince a man not to cleave to his wife, he will present another woman for that man to cleave to.

What if your husband cheated? How can you heal and your marriage be made whole again? One of the first things you need to know is adultery affects both parties involved. It hurts the victim the most, but it rips away at the soul of the offender. With that being said, you must understand that you have to heal together, instead of trying to heal individually. You and your spouse are one in the LORD, and the enemy was able to attack the two of you because you didn't cleave to one another. You didn't operate as one, therefore, if you heal individually, the divide will still be there, and the enemy will still have access to your marriage. Of course, this doesn't mean that you see and treat the husband as if he's been victimized. What it does mean is you encourage his healing as he encourages yours. The two of you absolutely have to come together and pray away any divide that may be in your marriage. At the same time, you have to get your friends and family members to understand that the two of you are one person, and as such, they should not be trying to divide you with their personal opinions, feelings, and perceptions. They need to encourage your healing as a unit rather than showing favoritism and placing a dividing line between the two of you.

If you've decided to stay with your husband, first and foremost, you have to get over the guilt associated with staying. In our society (and generation), it is not uncommon for the wives of adulterous husbands to be criticized, judged, and even mocked by people who don't understand their strength. Nevertheless, you have to remember that you're not married to them, and their opinions of you and your husband shouldn't have any weight in your marriage. Below are ten tips to surviving with your spouse after adultery has attacked your union.

1. **Keep GOD first.** Adultery divides a couple, and our pain will often cause us to focus so much on ourselves that we end up having trouble hearing from GOD. Don't put your emotions first, keep GOD first. Pray and continue to be led by HIM throughout it all.

2. **Understand that he may be hurting, too.** When we're victims, we see ourselves as victims and we look for the villains who've victimized us. Locating or identifying a villain helps us to justify remaining victims while we sort out our emotions. This isn't the best way to heal. Always remember that even though your husband was the villain, he's still your husband, and chances are, he does love you. He may feel bad about what he's done, and then again, he may have absolutely no conscience about it whatsoever. Either way, if you've decided to stay with him, you need to encourage his healing as he encourages yours.

3. **Forgive the husband.** The hardest thing to do is to forgive someone who's betrayed your trust, but forgiveness is vital to your healing. Ask GOD to put forgiveness in your heart for your husband, and then exercise that forgiveness until it becomes strong enough to activate itself. This means that you try to focus on your marriage rather than focusing on what happened and why it happened.
4. **Forgive the mistress.** You can't forgive the husband until you've forgiven the mistress. The reason is because every time you see or hear of her, you will associate her with your husband and this will enrage and hurt you all over again. Remember, she's a victim of her thinking and whatever else has happened to her over the course of her life. This isn't to justify her adulteries, but it is to say that GOD loves her and will forgive her if she repents and you should, too.
5. **Find new hobbies together.** When a

union has been attacked by adultery, many of the hobbies a couple had together are left behind when the couple decides to move ahead with their marriage. For this reason, it is always good to try and start life over again with your spouse, leaving behind old hobbies and starting new ones.
6. **See the husband and mistress as individuals, not as one.** How you view your husband and his ex-mistress will determine if your marriage is able to survive. If you continue to view them as a unit, even after they've split, you will have trouble cleaving to and trusting your husband again. Try not to refer to her as his mistress or ex-mistress; instead, try referring to her by her name, or better yet, if you can refrain from referring to her at all, that would be even better.
7. **Change your phone numbers.** Both parties should be willing to change their phone numbers, otherwise, the ex-mistress may be able to reach out yet again and stir

up some old emotions. Of course, if the wife didn't cheat and the mistress doesn't have her phone number, she should be allowed to keep her number, but the husband must absolutely be willing to change his number. Starting over again means starting afresh and giving the enemy no room to come between you.

8. **Toss out any and everything that reminds you of your husband's affair.** This includes that "guilt-gift" he likely purchased you while in the midst of his affair. This also includes any and all underwear he has and anything he may have worn while entertaining his mistress.

9. **Talk about it, but not too often.** Sure, the two of you should schedule time together to speak about what happened and the husband should answer any new questions you have to help with the healing process. Nevertheless, the actual healing won't start until the both of you put the affair behind you. This means that if you need three

months to talk about it, you won't start healing until after those three months are over. That's because every new question and answer will rip away at your heart. I advised the men to talk with their wives for one hour a day during the first month, but I advise you not to use every moment to talk about the affair. Don't keep asking the same questions using different words. Let it go and accept whatever answers he gives to you until GOD shows you otherwise.

10. **Seek Christian counseling.** I know it's embarrassing (especially for the husband) to tell your pastor about what the two of you have just survived, but talking about it with someone who may stand in as a mediator may help speed up the healing process.

11. **Change the channel.** I know that watching movies about men who cheat on their wives may seem like a good idea when your emotions are stirred up, but they won't help you heal. Instead, they'll only stir you up more and instigate a fight between you and

your spouse. Change the channel and watch uplifting and encouraging movies that help lend to your future together rather than remind you of your past.

12. **Change the station.** You turn on the radio and your favorite song comes on. All of a sudden, you find yourself speeding down the highway teary-eyed and thinking about what you're going to say to your husband when you get home. Stop it! Change the station. Listen to music that encourages and uplifts you, preferably gospel music.

13. **Cast down evil imaginations.** I know that adulterous imaginations can haunt you to torments, but you have power over your mind. You get to say what plays in your head and what has to stop. Stop entertaining thoughts of what your husband did and start imagining a great future together.

14. **Bind the spirit of idolatry before you bind the spirit of adultery.** The two of you should come together as one and go into

warfare, and remember, your husband committed idolatry first.

15. **Don't forget about GOD.** GOD was hurt the most in your husband's affair, so don't cut HIM out. Use this as an opportunity to bring HIM in even more.

16. **Exercise.** When you're upset, try going for a brisk jog and talking to the LORD about how you feel. If your husband tags along, that's great. If not, use that time to pray and get past your negative emotions. Exercising causes your body to release endorphins, and these endorphins trigger positive moods.

17. **Don't try to sex "her" away.** One of the most common responses to an adulterous affair is sex. All too often, the wives of adulterers will try to sex the other woman off their husbands by initiating many sexual encounters with their husbands or by changing their sexual personality altogether. Remember, his strongman was sexual perversion, so feeding the

strongman with more sex won't cause it to go away. Your husband needs to be delivered and have his mind renewed, so don't try to use sex to win your husband's heart again.

18. **Start expressing your love for one another in unique ways.** Marriage can become boring quite easily when the individuals involved become predictable and monotonous. Be unpredictable and share your love with your husband in ways outside of sex. Email him, leave love letters around the house, engage in playtime with him, or take time out each day to compliment him. Of course, this doesn't guarantee he will be faithful, but what it does do is build your husband up. If he chooses to fall again, your hands will be clean.

19. **Remain unified all the days of your life.** You and your husband are one in the eyes of the LORD, but the enemy is going to try to divide you. His favorite weapon against

a couple is pride and self-pity. Keep those two strongmen out of your marriage and you'll find that peace will abide in your home. Sit down and talk about what the two of you intend to do to remain unified. Remember, a country doesn't prepare for war in times of war, countries prepare for war in times of peace. That way, their enemies don't catch them off guard and overtake them. Prepare for any attacks against your marriage in times of peace. Discuss your ways of escape and encourage your spouse (and he should do the same for you) to talk to you about anything that's bothering, haunting, or tempting him at any given time. When he has an open door to speak with you without fear of retaliation or negative emotions, you will have closed one of the doors the enemy used to speak to him.

20. **Reclaim your marriage.** Adultery doesn't just impact a marriage, adultery often takes authority over that marriage. The two of

> you should stand as one and reclaim your marriage rather than allowing the spirit of adultery to reign over it.

When adultery enters the picture, the odds are against your marriage. Adultery is a strongman that has proven itself to be stronger than many marriages. After all, every marriage has its strengths and weaknesses. A marriage is only as strong as the people in it. And just as adultery has destroyed many marriages, the spirit of pride has also caused many marriages to fail. A common example is: a wife discovers her husband's indiscretions and demands that he call off his affair. The husband complies and works hard to restore his marriage to his wife, but his wife's pride won't allow her to remain in that marriage. It's not that she can't be with him, the issue is that adultery went outside of her conditions or limitations. Another common example is: a wife discovers her husband's adulterous affair, and demands that he call it off. The husband, being filled with pride, refuses to end the affair because he doesn't like being told what to do. Therefore, adultery and pride usually work together to destroy marriages, and for this reason, GOD commands us to not allow either of these strongmen in our hearts, homes or marriages.

Matthew 5:28: But I say unto you, That whosoever looketh on a woman to lust after her hath committed adultery with her already in his heart.

Proverbs 16:18: Pride goeth before destruction, and an haughty spirit before a fall.

One mistake many women make is telling anyone who will listen about their husband's indiscretions. I've heard many men say that they'd begged their wives for forgiveness, and had done many things to prove to their wives that they were sorrowful about their past indiscretions, only to have their wives reject them before serving them with divorce papers. The reason for such behavior is: all too often, women (especially young women) will get their friends and family involved because they don't know how to handle all of the emotions they are experiencing. After they'd spoken reproachfully about their husbands to their loved ones, many women were surprised by how emotionally involved their loved ones had become in their marriages. Their marriages then became public domain, where everyone who was confided in felt they suddenly had the right to voice their opinions in regard to that marriage. When the husband repents to the wife for his affair, she may feel obligated to remain emotionally in agreement with the people who've supported and encouraged her when she was broken. After all, none of them have ever hurt her at the capacity in which her husband has hurt her and their support has caused her to give them vested interest in her marriage. A private apology from her husband in such a case will likely not be accepted because the problem is not a private one anymore, it's public domain. In such a case, the wife will likely expect her husband to issue a public apology to her so everyone who's involved won't become angry with or judge her if she decides to reconcile with her husband and emotionally recommit herself to that marriage. This may be foolish on her part, but we have to understand that everyone handles their emotions differently because we all have our varied degrees of strength. All the same, it is understandable that she'd want to stick by the people who have supported her, and any man who is truly repentant won't have a problem giving her what she needs to recommit herself to that marriage. But again, pride will often get in the way of such a reconciliation because one or both parties involved will likely misinterpret the other's behavior and respond to what they think their spouses are attempting to do rather than responding to what their spouses are actually trying to do.

The key to surviving an adulterous affair together is truth because everything the two of you do and say will be an action that inspires a reaction. Both parties should be open to communicating with one another, regardless of how uncomfortable those communications are, and both parties should be willing to speak truthfully with one another. That's because the truth is a light that cannot be concealed, but will make itself known, whereas, lies are darkness that are always exposed by the light of truth.

Below are ten additional tips and recaps to surviving an adulterous affair together.

1. **Don't lose friends trying to keep your husband, and don't lose your husband trying to keep your friends.** First and foremost, you shouldn't tell any and everyone what you're going through because everyone has their own measure of faith and their own degree of tolerance. Once you get people involved, they will remain involved, and if you try to exclude them, you run the risk of losing their friendships.

2. **Take your healing one day at a time.** The problem with us is we often try to rush our healing because we want to return to our normal lives, but you can't rush the stages of grief. You have to allow the situation to

play out and you have to heal day by day until your healing is complete. Additionally, returning to your normal life may prove to be fatal to your marriage. Instead, the two of you should build new lives together, rather than trying to rebuild the old one.

3. **Communication is key.** Most marriages that end because of adultery ended because one or both parties involved refused to communicate. Sit down and talk about it. Make plans together to overcome the adultery rather than remaining divided. Sure, the husband may be the offender, but that doesn't mean GOD approves of division in your home. If you want to be together, you have to respond to adultery together.

4. **Respect is the first door communication opens.** One of the worst blows to a marriage is when a wife loses respect for her husband or vice versa. Once respect is gone, communication will crumble and indignation will slowly start to seep in. Yes,

it's more than difficult to respect a man who's lain with another woman, but GOD specifically tells wives to respect their husbands (See Ephesians 5:33). Just remember that trust and respect are different, even though they are interchangeable. To respect him means that you continue to honor GOD by honoring him. Let him talk and don't speak evil at him; instead, win him with your behavior, not your words.

5. **Let the past be the past.** This one is probably the hardest of them all because when we're hurt, we want to talk about what's hurting us so the pain will go away. Needless to say, communication is good, but repeating a matter is the quickest way to cut the lines of communication. Rather than confront the husband about his past affairs once again, the best thing to do is confront your feelings. Go into another room and pray or cry. You can even write a note to your husband expressing how you

feel, and then, ball that note up once you're done. This will help you to release those feelings without instigating a fight with your husband. Don't keep bringing up the past. Doing so won't keep the husband from re-offending you. Instead, look toward your future together.

6. **Forgive on purpose.** Forgiveness isn't a feeling you just wait on. Forgiveness isn't a feeling at all, it's a heart condition, and it's a choice. We choose to forgive just as we choose not to forgive. Regardless of whether you stay with your husband or not, you must forgive him if you want GOD to forgive you of your sins. To forgive him doesn't mean that you trust him, it simply means you accept what CHRIST JESUS did for him on the cross. HE forgave your husband if your husband repented. Now, you must do the same. Ask GOD to put forgiveness in your heart for your husband, and then, you must activate and exercise that forgiveness by walking in it. This

means you can't keep bringing up the past if you expect to have a future together.

7. **Get rid of anything that has bad memories attached to it.** The healing process can sometimes be lengthy, and for this reason, you should never delay your healing by keeping things around that remind you of your husband's affair or his mistress. If you wore your favorite red shirt the day you caught your husband with his mistress, and now that shirt reminds you of that day, get rid of that shirt. If your husband was wearing his designer blue jeans when he went to see his mistress, he ought to get rid of those jeans. Material things are tangible and can easily be replaced, but peace is intangible and can sometimes be elusive.

8. **Start new hobbies together.** Any time you try to "pick up where you left off", you may find yourself being reminded of your husband's affair. Create new dreams and hobbies together so the two of you can

make a fresh start.

9. **Don't try to help anyone else going through what you've been through until you've completely healed.** You can help while you're going through it, but you shouldn't help when you've started the healing process. I wanted to write this book almost immediately after Roger and I broke up, but, of course, GOD wasn't going to allow that because I was still in the process of healing. It is only when you've healed and forgiven the person who's hurt you that you can successfully help others heal and forgive the people who've hurt them.

10. **Pray together every day and don't allow division to ever come into your marriage (or home) again.** A house divided cannot stand; we know this. But what most people don't realize is that adultery is often the result of a house divided. Constantly disagreeing with one another only opens the door for other people to come into your marriage. Sure, we all have differences of

opinion, but, in marriage, we have to learn to respect one another's opinions and not try to always burden our spouses with our own opinions. That's why communication is key, and being willing to give and take makes for an impenetrable marriage. Decide to pray together, talk together, war together, and stand together, and it is then and only then, that your marriage will become a weapon against the kingdom of darkness.

Your marriage can survive and the two of you can go on to be happy with one another once again. It simply requires two people who've made up their minds that their marriages will work and they are willing to put the necessary time and effort into making those marriages work. At the same time, marriage is an institution designed by GOD, so you can't shut HIM out of it. Instead, you need HIM to be the glue that holds your marriage together. Adultery is hurtful, but it's something that many women have endured and survived, and you can, too. Don't see this as the end of you or your marriage, see it as an opportunity for GOD to show HIMSELF as all powerful. I survived two marriages that had been damaged and destroyed by adultery, and even though my marriages ended in divorce, I know many people who've remained together after their spouses committed adultery. And I'm glad I endured what I've endured because it taught me so much about myself and helped me to seek healing in places I didn't realize I needed healing. All the same, it caused me to exercise my forgiveness muscles until I became so strong, I was able to keep my peace in the midst of a broken marriage. I chose to forgive and I chose to be happy. I cried, I raged, and I felt as if I wouldn't live to see another day, but GOD brought me through without a scratch on my heart. I'm all new again and I've learned the lessons I needed to learn. Today, I don't just see the light at the end of the tunnel, that light now lives in me. Just make up your mind that you won't faint or allow your emotions to consume you. Make up your mind that you will be happy one day, whether it's with the husband you have now or the husband GOD will appoint for you later...should your current husband refuse to humble himself and repent. There is power in a made up mind. Tap into that power and just keep living...better days are coming, and one day (if you do not faint), you will look back and testify about what GOD brought you through rather than complaining about what your husband took you through.

How GOD Deals with an Adulterous Husband

We know GOD wants us to be still and trust HIM when we're in the midst of a storm. Knowing what to do isn't the problem. The issue is applying what we know to our situations. That's because adultery is one of the most painful experiences a spouse can endure. Again, it is so painful that it is one of the three ways GOD permits us out of a marriage. The three legal ways to get out of a marriage are:

- **Adultery/ Fornication**
  (See Matthew 19:9)
- **If the Unbelieving Spouse Leaves**
  (See 1 Corinthians 7:15)
- **Death**
  (See 1 Corinthians 7:29)

One of the reasons most believing wives have trouble letting GOD deal with their adulterous

How God Deals with an Adulterous Husband

husbands is because we are all moved by what we see until we get enough faith to secure us. When a husband is committing adultery against his wife, he is so far outside of the will of GOD, he will center his every move around his lusts or selfish desires rather than thinking logically. That's because a double-minded man is unstable in all his ways (See James 1:8). On one hand, he knows he wants to be with his wife, but on the other hand, he's overwhelmed by his dark thoughts and fiery lusts toward the other woman or other women. Because of this, he will be unstable, moody, and unpredictable. He doesn't know what he wants to do, and when he feels pressured to make a decision about his wife or his mistress, he could become even more unstable. At the same time, he's full of voids, and these voids have been created through his associations (peers), lack of relationship with GOD, or his disobedience to the WORD of GOD (rebellion). The further away from GOD a man becomes, the more selfish and unsympathetic he will become, and that's because his unrepentant heart caused

How God Deals with an Adulterous Husband

him to erect himself as his own idol. When dealing with an adulterous man, you will notice he will constantly refer to himself, how he feels, what he wants, and what he thinks he's not getting. He will often see his wife's pain as an attack against his peace, and will therefore, find it difficult to console or empathize with the woman he's vowed to love and protect. When his wife cries, he doesn't see her pain; instead, he sees her tears as an attack against his plans. He may become enraged because, in his mind, he believes his affair shouldn't be such a big issue; after all, he's coming home to his wife. He's paying bills at home, and if the wife has children from a previous relationship, he may see her as ungrateful when responding to his adulteries. All too often, his thoughts are:

- *I'm raising another man's children.*
- *I've done more for her kids than their own daddy has done!*
- *I didn't want a woman with kids, but I accepted her kids, and now, she has the nerve to complain.*

How God Deals with an Adulterous Husband

His problem is, he's become self-righteous and the enemy will try to help him stay in his adulteries by causing him to see himself as a blessing to his wife as opposed to looking at the curse he's operating under. Men who unrepentantly commit adultery will often look at the good things they've done for their wives rather than acknowledging that what they've done is their own responsibility as husbands. By seeing themselves as victims and their wives as ungrateful women who don't mind benefiting from them, many adulterers will grow to resent their wives. The enemy's three step program works this way:

1. Cause the husband to find a problem in the marriage and focus on it.
2. Cause the husband to see himself as a "good thing" and to see his wife as a selfish and bothersome woman who's "holding him back".
3. Cause the husband to pity himself and see himself as a victim who deserves better.

That's where the other woman comes in. She

How God Deals with an Adulterous Husband

offers the straying husband the opportunity to feel wanted, but her most powerful weapon is the ability to help him feel needed. You see, a wife will often become comfortable with her husband, and because she loves and respects him, she may unknowingly take on too many responsibilities, causing her husband to feel unneeded. A man must absolutely feel needed to feel secure, just as a woman must feel protected and safe to feel secure.

The other woman learns what her prey feels he isn't getting at home, and she zeros in on his voids. She will manipulate the man into thinking she is moral, empathetic, loving, and fragile. If that man's wife is moral, empathetic, loving, and fragile, the mistress may manipulate him into thinking she's the fun-loving, extroverted, and free spirit he's missing at home. In other words, she will become everything he thinks he needs, and because he's not getting from his wife what he believes he's getting from his mistress, he will begin to distance himself from his wife. He may begin to see his wife as a curse or an obstacle,

How God Deals with an Adulterous Husband

and because of this perception, he will purposely sabotage his marriage. In most cases, when a man leaves his wife to be with his mistress, he comes to realize how much his wife added to him once he's put her away. Once the mistress becomes the center of that man's world, it is only then that she realizes how much of a burden the man is she's seduced through her adulteries. She then finds herself in his wife's old shoes, and because she's immoral, she will likely end the relationship or become extremely insecure while in that relationship. She will become a thorn in that man's side.

GOD deals with adulterers by allowing them to have what they think they want. You have to understand that there are no blessings in sin, and, of course, GOD knows this. The wife may not realize this because it's not uncommon for the enemy to tell her that her estranged husband is off with his new mistress and they're happy while she's miserable, but the truth is, most relationships are great in the beginning. All the same, forbidden

How God Deals with an Adulterous Husband

fruit doesn't always taste better, it only tastes different. When someone bites into adultery, they will often want to return to that fruit because it's not familiar to them. It isn't until the husband becomes used to his mistress that he begins to see her for what she is. A man who rarely gets to see and sex his mistress will often become obsessed with the mistress because of her inaccessibility, but a man who sees and sexes his mistress often will likely tire of her rather quickly. For this reason, many mistresses have learned to tease their adulterous lovers, playing on a man's natural need to hunt something. They'll rarely have sex with their lovers, and they won't allow their lovers to have full access to them at all times. Men are hunters by nature, so for an adulterous man, such behavior will always pique his curiosity and even cause him to think the sex with his mistress is better because it's something he rarely gets. It's similar to how we were as children. We thought a cheeseburger from a restaurant was better than the food at home because we rarely went out to eat. For most of us, after we'd grown

How God Deals with an Adulterous Husband

up and had numerous cheeseburgers on our lunch breaks, we'd come to realize how much better the food at home is. By allowing a man to have what he thinks he wants, GOD shows that man just what sin has in store for him. A straying husband will walk so far down the path of adultery that he'll leave behind so many of the treasures he's accomplished in his life, and one of those treasures is his relationship with his children. He reaches a dead end and realizes that adultery hadn't taken him far into the blessings the enemy promised him, but had, instead, taken him far away from the blessings GOD had given him. When he looks back, he notices how beautiful, blessed, and favored his estranged or ex wife is; meaning, he is no longer blinded by the lies the enemy told him. That's because Satan wants him to see how foolish he was. Satan wants him to see how much damage he's done to his family because Satan wants to destroy that man. He didn't send the mistress to bless him, she came to destroy him. He comes to realize that he's left love to pursue lust, and lust is nothing more than a

How God Deals with an Adulterous Husband

demonic impersonation of love. The enemy will use that man's choices against him, and begin to tell him that he's stupid, useless, and hell bound. He may even cause that man to become bitter with his now estranged wife or ex-wife because the enemy will remind him that she is a good woman. The enemy will taunt him and torment his mind, telling him that his ex will now go on to be blessed and make some man happy, and she has all of his stuff (houses, cars, children) to make some man a very happy man. That's when most men who've lost their wives because of their adulterous relationships begin to lash out against their exes by requesting custody of the children or demanding more time with their children. It isn't the children they're after. They want second chances with the women they've abandoned, and when rejected by those women, many estranged husbands and ex-husbands become even more unstable. Some even become suicidal or homicidal maniacs. Of course, when we're in the LORD and we refuse to come outside of HIS will, we are protected by GOD.

How God Deals with an Adulterous Husband

GOD doesn't allow that man to feel those things because HE wants to destroy him (because HE doesn't), but he allows him to experience the wages of sin so he can fully repent. The wages of sin is death, and the death of that man's marriage may prove to be something he doesn't feel he can get past. Of course, the LORD offers him a chance to reconcile himself with GOD, and eventually become a better husband to his estranged wife, or if the marriage has ended, to maybe remarry one day and be a better husband to his new wife than he was to the former one. GOD then teaches him about the spirit of an adulteress, and shows him how he'd been sucked into a life of lusts and lies that led him down a path that would have killed him had he not repented. You see, there is so much to learn about an adulteress, and if a man does not know what her purpose is, he will see her the way the enemy wants him to see her. Once he wakes up to the truth, however, he will come to understand that everyone in the realm of the earth has a purpose, and the purpose of the adulteress is to reduce

How God Deals with an Adulterous Husband

him, or cause him to fall before exposing him to the enemy to be destroyed.

Proverbs 6:26: For by means of a whorish woman a man is brought to a piece of bread: and the adulteress will hunt for the precious life.

When a man cheats, he also steps out from under the order as arranged by GOD, and that order is published in 1 Corinthians 11:3: "But I would have you know, that the head of every man is Christ; and the head of the woman is the man; and the head of Christ is God." The straying husband rejects his covering (CHRIST JESUS) to walk in the lusts and lies the enemy has set before him. His wife, on the other hand, must seek to remain covered through CHRIST by not retaliating or allowing herself to become vengeful and unforgiving. By staying in the will of GOD, she remains protected and covered by the LORD. The LORD will use a willing wife to win her husband to HIM, and this is accomplished only when the wife is willing to get past her emotions and refrain from constantly arguing with her husband. What the

How God Deals with an Adulterous Husband

LORD is doing is using that wife to reflect HIMSELF through to the husband who's gone astray. This doesn't guarantee the husband will repent and give up his ways, it simply gives GOD an opportunity to extend a way of escape to the husband, as well as an opportunity to repent. If the husband chooses to continue in his adulteries, he will reject his wife in the same hour that he rejects his GOD. By rejecting the wife, the husband loses his favor from GOD. By rejecting GOD, he rejects everything GOD stands for, and he stands in danger of becoming declared lukewarm, and as such, CHRIST said HE would spit him out of HIS mouth. This means that HE will reject the man who has rejected HIS FATHER. Any time you see a man who's taken this path and not repented, you will notice how weary his soul has become because sin has waged war against his mind. You will notice how his finances are always under attack, his health is always under attack, and his peace has evaded him. It's not because of what he's done that he's so far away from being blessed, it's because he refuses to

How God Deals with an Adulterous Husband

repent for what he's done. We've all sinned and fallen short of GOD'S glory, but HE is faithful and just to forgive us our sins, and to cleanse us from all unrighteousness if we confess our sins (See 1 John 1:9).

If a man repents, on the other hand, GOD is faithful and merciful enough to forgive him. Of course, he will still deal with many of the repercussions from his choices, but GOD will extend mercy to him. For example, at the beginning of my relationship with Taylor, we'd committed adultery because he was still yet married to his first wife. He was going through a divorce. I tried to justify my actions with the fact that I'd met him after the divorce had been set in motion; nevertheless, even after apologizing to GOD, I still had to live with my choices. Taylor committed adultery with me, and therefore, we were both adulterers. For this reason, he didn't know how to be faithful to me because I'd gotten with him the wrong way. When I met Roger, I was going through a divorce from Taylor, and one

How God Deals with an Adulterous Husband

would've thought I'd learned my lesson, but I hadn't. I still tried to justify my actions, and because I committed adultery to get Roger, I ended up marrying an adulterer. After all, I was an adulteress, and we usually attract what we are. While in the midst of my marriage to Roger, I stopped apologizing and I actually repented. When Roger and I went through our divorce, I didn't date, court, or entertain any man; instead, I had recommitted myself to GOD so much that I'd banned the idea of fornication from my heart. I denounced adultery and I denounced fornication and declared over myself that the only man who would have my hand in marriage would be the man GOD has given permission to marry me. Once I truly repented, I was no longer an adulteress, and I was able to recommit myself to GOD. GOD forgave me for the adulteries I'd committed, therefore, it would be foolish for me to think HE couldn't forgive Taylor or Roger. I want HIM to forgive them because HE forgave me. You ought to have that same attitude toward your husband. Yes, what he did was wrong, and yes,

How God Deals with an Adulterous Husband

adultery is one of the worst things a man can take his wife through, but it's not an unforgivable sin. You just have to will in within your heart to forgive him, and remember, forgiveness is a Godly concept, meaning, it stands outside of our natural understanding and must be acquired through faith. Forgiveness isn't a feeling you get, it's a renewed mind because you no longer look at the person and see someone who's hurt you. Instead, you see them as a new creature. This doesn't mean they won't cheat again, but what it does mean is that you're taking on the attitude of GOD in relation to them. When CHRIST died for us, HIS death didn't stop us from sinning, but what it did was extended forgiveness to us for our past, present, and future sins. This doesn't give us the license to sin, but it gives us the room to be human, and GOD'S grace gives us the opportunity to repent for our slip-ups. Does this mean that we can all go out and sin against GOD and use the grace of GOD to excuse ourselves? No, because rebellion is a sin of witchcraft. What it means is GOD understands that we are not perfect

How God Deals with an Adulterous Husband

creatures, and we will fall short of HIS glory from time to time. HE knows our sins aren't always intentional. For example, it's a sin to worry. It's also a sin to doubt GOD. The grace of GOD gives us the time we need to get to know GOD better so we can become better people. It's not an excuse to sin, just as forgiving your husband does not give him the right to go out and sin against you once again.

When dealing with an adulterer, GOD has to get him to the point where he not only apologizes for what he's done, but he repents. To apologize simply means to say or verbally express one's sorrow for having done or said something, but to repent means to turn your heart back to GOD. To repent means you denounce the sin itself and pursue the kingdom of GOD and all its righteousness. To repent means to put away or divorce the sin so you can remain married to GOD. Some men realize their wrongs and repent almost immediately; whereas, others have to go through intense trials and tribulations to get them

How God Deals with an Adulterous Husband

to finally denounce their adulterous ways and follow the paths GOD has set before them. Every adulterous husband is a Jonah, wherewith, they have chosen to flee from the will of GOD, but their choices to do so will cause them to be swallowed up by a whale. Their whale may not live in the ocean. Sometimes, one man's whale is the destruction of his marriage, whereas, another man's whale is the destruction of his flesh. One man's whale may be financial devastation, and another man's whale is total humiliation. It goes without saying, one man's whale may be larger than another man's whale, and the reason for this is because of the mantle on that guy's life. A man who is called or chosen by GOD to carry out an assignment in the earth is a man who can't afford to tempt sin because his whale may be the destruction of his marriage, flesh, finances, and total humiliation. His testimony will have to match the size of his sin. GOD will always get HIS point across, but it's always up to the man whom HE is communicating with to hear and hearken to HIS voice. A man who turns his head when GOD speaks to him is the same man who will call out to GOD and not be heard.

What GOD wants from you is your total cooperation with HIM as HE attempts to reach your husband. HE wants you to pray for your husband, stand in the gap for him, and put away strife from you so that sin won't lead you astray as well. HE needs a vessel in that home to reach the man whose heart has been taken captive by a seducing spirit, and if you're willing, GOD will show you how powerful HE is. HE will prove to you that HE is Almighty. There will be days when it may all feel too overwhelming, but those days usually indicate that you're so close to GOD, the devil has begun to lash out against you. It also means that you have the perfect opportunity to take a bad situation and hand it over to the LORD right in the devil's face. You see, the devil expects you to get emotional and sin against GOD with your words or your actions, but when you use that opportunity to obey GOD instead, you will cause the enemy to flee from you in fear. If you decide

How God Deals with an Adulterous Husband

to stay, treat your husband with love and respect. If you decide to leave, treat your husband with love and respect. It's not up to you to avenge yourself, that's a job only GOD can perform. When we stay in our appointed seats and let GOD sit on HIS throne, we are in the same taking a situation that could have lasted for decades and serving it with eviction papers. When you obey GOD, you put a time limit on the enemy, but when you disobey GOD, you give the enemy an extended stay in your home, life, and finances. When you obey GOD and refuse to allow your emotions to mislead you, you will cause the enemy to flee from you, and at the same time, you are giving your husband a choice: he can either repent and stay with you (if that's what you want), or you can ask the devil to take him with him as he flees the scene.

Know this: GOD doesn't need your help to correct your husband, HE simply needs your cooperation. Pray and ask HIM each and every day to keep you and to protect you. Obey every Word HE sends your way, and HE will prove to you why HE is El

How God Deals with an Adulterous Husband

Shaddai (GOD Almighty).

Effective Warfare Tactics

Any time I'm counseling a woman who's married to an adulterer and seeking help with her marriage, I listen to her to get a better understanding of what she wants. Does she want the marriage to work or does she want a divorce? Of course, I know I'm more than likely not going to tell her what she wants to hear, but knowing what she wants helps me to deliver the truth to her in a way that won't overwhelm her. In most cases, I've found that the wife wanted the mistress out of the picture and she wanted her marriage to be repaired. I've also found that many wives blame the entire destruction of their marriages on the mistresses involved, and saw their husbands as nothing more than simple men ensnared by crafty women. So, first things first, I have to work on helping them to understand that an adulteress is an adulteress, and if their husbands weren't adulterers, they wouldn't have committed adultery

Effective Warfare Tactics

with those women. The problem isn't the adulteress; the problem is always the husband, unless, of course, he was forcibly raped. *If he's committing adultery, we know he wasn't raped; he was a willing participant in the destruction of his marriage.*

One of the reasons I first attempt to change the wife's perception is because she can't effectively pray against the spirits behind adultery until she accepts the truth. The truth is:
1. Her husband committed adultery because he wanted to commit adultery.
2. The mistress isn't the devil's bride, she's an adulteress, and as such, she needs to be prayed for, not raged against.
3. An adulteress cannot successfully seduce a faithful man.
4. Every affair wasn't initiated by the other woman. In most cases, it's the husband who initiated the affair.
5. Praying against the mistress is a prayer gone amiss. Praying for her, on the other

Effective Warfare Tactics

hand, is a prayer GOD will honor.

Taking her focus off the other woman helps her to better zero in on the spirits that have somehow entered into her home and attacked her marriage. **Ephesians 6:12:** For we wrestle not against flesh and blood, but against principalities, against powers, against the rulers of the darkness of this world, against spiritual wickedness in high places.

Let's face it, the enemy is everywhere, and he will use whomever he can to bring down a marriage. It's up to the married couple as individuals and as a united front to stay on the righteous path that's been carved for them by JESUS CHRIST. When we go out of our doors each and every day, we walk into the very midst of murderers, rapists, adulterers, whoremongers, sorcerers, witches, blasphemers, slanderers, and the like. The key is to not allow these people or their spirits into our homes, nor should we learn their ways. This means we have to successfully leave our homes to do whatever we've set out to do, and return home not having brought any of the spirits walking about the earth with us. The devil cannot come into your home unless you invite him, and he'll use anyone he can to get an invitation into your home or marriage. He'll use your relatives, co-workers, and even your own spouse to wage war against your marriage. An adulteress is just one of the tools he uses, therefore, to focus on her is error. To be angry with her, you would have to be angry with every adulteress in this world, and there are millions (if not billions) of them. That's too many people to be mad at. All the same, you have to be angry with the adulterer who invited her into your marriage. An adulteress doesn't just sleep with another woman's husband, an adulteress is judgment manifested. She is a temptress and a seducing spirit, and her assignment (from the enemy) is to divide the "one" (couple) and make them two. When we are one with our spouses, our unions are impenetrable to the enemy because of our united front. When the enemy can get a man to think individually, he can persuade that man to think apart from his wife, meaning he

Effective Warfare Tactics

will no longer care what his wife says or thinks. He will see himself as a victim of her bad attitude or wrongful thinking, and as such, he will begin to see himself as the one who's been victimized by her for far too long. To him, the mistress represents a get-away or a retreat in human form. She's the escape he's come to enjoy, and even though the truth will wage war against the lies he's allowed in his heart, he will often ignore the truth or override it with the lies he's been telling himself. What this means is, he's under attack and he doesn't realize it because the seductress is distracting him while the devil positions him for destruction.

For this reason, the wife has every right to intercede for her husband and to wage war against the enemy. By doing so, she is telling the enemy that he is not welcome in her home or marriage. Needless to say, for her to successfully wage war against the enemy, she has to take her focus off the mistress and the current state of her husband. She then has to focus on the spirits

Effective Warfare Tactics

behind the attack, and this isn't easy to do because a woman with a broken heart has trouble seeing anything but the people who have broken her heart. Because of this, it is always wise for her to get her pastor and other believers involved in praying for her. Of course, she should ask GOD who she can turn to for intercession, and the people will all come together and wage war against the devil.

Matthew 18:20: For where two or three are gathered together in my name, there am I in the midst of them.

2 Corinthians 13:1: This is the third time I am coming to you. In the mouth of two or three witnesses shall every word be established.

James 4:7: Submit yourselves therefore to God. Resist the devil, and he will flee from you.

First and foremost, do not begin to entertain witchcraft disguised as Christian warfare tactics. For example, I've come across a few believers who believe that putting salt in front of their doors will keep the devil out. This lie roots itself in

Effective Warfare Tactics

Southern hoodoo and should never be a part of a Christian's lifestyle. It goes without saying that everyone I've come across who practices leaving salt at their front doors is not surprisingly always under attack. Turning to psychics and diviners is also pure and unadulterated witchcraft and those who do such a thing set themselves up for destruction.

Leviticus 20:6: And the soul that turneth after such as have familiar spirits, and after wizards, to go a whoring after them, I will even set my face against that soul, and will cut him off from among his people.

1 Chronicles 10:13-14: So Saul died for his transgression which he committed against the LORD, even against the word of the LORD, which he kept not, and also for asking counsel of one that had a familiar spirit, to inquire of it; and inquired not of the LORD: therefore he slew him, and turned the kingdom unto David the son of Jesse.

How can you effectively wage war against a devil

Effective Warfare Tactics

you cannot see? After all, most women wage war against the man they can see and the women that man is seeing. Below are some very effective warfare tactics and tips:

1. Anoint your home with holy oil and decree and declare what can and cannot enter into your home. I did this the same night Roger left. While he was at work, I took my oil through the bedroom he'd been sleeping in and I anointed the bed, that room, and my entire apartment. I declared that neither the devil nor his angels could come into my apartment or sleep in that bed. I commanded the warring angels of GOD to arrest any devil, power, or principality that entered or attempted to enter my home, and cast those wicked spirits into the abyss until the day of judgment. When Roger came home, he put one foot in the front door and pulled it back out. He stood in the doorway yelling at me about something I'd thrown away, and he finally came into the place to pack his bags. Needless to say, he

Effective Warfare Tactics

came into the house, packed his bags in less than thirty minutes, and left in a hurry.
2. Do not trust any anointing oil given to you by someone you don't know, because you don't know what's been spoken over that oil. If you have a church home and you *know* that GOD is with your pastor, you can ask him for some anointing oil. At the same time, you can make your own. Simply go to the store and buy some virgin olive oil and pray over it. It's not the oil that's effective, its' the faith you have in GOD to work through that oil that makes it powerful.
3. When you're feeling emotional, don't wage war against your husband. He's flesh and blood, so warfare is ineffective against him. Instead, go into warfare against the spirits that are tormenting you. Waging war against the man only awakens his flesh, but engaging in warfare against the spirits in or seducing the man is how you win the war.
4. Intercede on behalf of the mistress or mistresses. The problem is, most women

Effective Warfare Tactics

pray against the mistress, not understanding that they aren't fighting against flesh and blood. When you pray for her deliverance and wage war against the spirits that are in or seducing her, you will then become a threat to the enemy because you're not just threatening to get your husband set free, but you are attempting to set free the woman or women the enemy is using to ruin your marriage. *That's something he didn't see coming.* The enemy does not want to lose her because, more than likely, he's used her to bring down other marriages before, or he wants to continue to use her. He then comes to realize that he stands at risk of losing her if he keeps her engaged. He may decide to pull her out, but this doesn't mean the war is over. The war is only over once your husband has repented of his adultery and his idolatry.

5. Fast. Fasting is one of the most effective weapons against the spirit of adultery

because you are humbling yourself before GOD and refusing to be led by your flesh. To fast is to tear down the flesh by refusing to strengthen it with food. This takes the battle from being one launched by your husband against you to being a war launched by the enemy against GOD, and the devil has already lost that fight.

6. Pray over your children. All too often, the children are overlooked when one of the parents commit adultery, and that's because most parents don't think they're affected by the affair. The truth is, children are very much so affected by adultery, as it affects their stability, their perception of their parents, and their self-perception. Often, children blame themselves for the failing of their parents' marriages, and this leads to a child becoming rebellious and withdrawn. Pray for your children and cover them with the blood of JESUS. Talk with them and let them know that whatever is going on between their father and

Effective Warfare Tactics

yourself is not their fault. More importantly, try not to argue or discuss your husband's infidelities around your children. There are a lot of women who try to involve their children because they want to their children to side with tehm, and at the same time, they want to send a message to the father through the children. That message is: *if you don't want our mother, you're going to lose us as well.* Putting a child in this position is not only foolish, but it can ruin your child's life.

7. Talk to GOD for real. It's not uncommon for a wife to talk around her husband in hopes that he will hear her and realize how severe their situation is. That's ineffective. A man hears only what he wants to hear, and he'll do what he wants to do, and therefore, telling your friends or family about your husband's indiscretions while in his presence will only work against you. Talk to GOD and keep your communications with your husband pure.

Effective Warfare Tactics

8. Do not trust any and everyone to intercede on behalf of your marriage. At one point in time, I'd opened up my marriage to Roger to anyone in ministry because I was in a lot of pain and I needed some direction. Needless to say, I ended up opening my marriage to the wrong people and this only intensified the warfare. Ask GOD who you can speak with and who can stand in the gap for you. Some people won't pray GOD'S will, they will send up their opinions in prayer form, only to have those prayers go amiss because they weren't praying GOD'S will. They were praying for their own will to be done.
9. Become the guiltless party. Most adulterous men need to feel justified in their behaviors, so they'll start arguments, and these arguments aren't just designed to help them get out of their houses for a few hours or a few days. Oftentimes, these arguments are designed to help them feel as if their wives *deserve* what they're

Effective Warfare Tactics

putting them through. We often play into this by allowing our emotions to get the best of us. When your husband steps on the battlefield, don't go out there to war with him. Instead, send the WORD after him. Be kind to him, even when he's being cruel to you. Pray for him, even when you don't want to. Take away his justification and it'll distract him from his mistress and get his focus back on you. The truth is, praise confuses the enemy when he was expecting war.

10. Do something nice for your husband when he least deserves it. Remember, the battlefield is in a man's mind, so you don't wage war against him by arguing with him. You wage war against the enemy by challenging your husband's thoughts. Go out and buy something nice for your husband. When you give it to him, simply say, "I'm giving you this because I love you." That's it! Don't say another word; don't mention what he's been doing and

Effective Warfare Tactics

don't talk about the problems in your marriage. What you're doing is leaving him alone to argue within himself rather than you being the one he argues with.

11. Don't change your look, change your attitude. One of the most common ways women respond to adultery is by changing their outward appearance. Wives will often change their hair or go on a diet in their attempts to win their husbands back. Here's the problem with this type of thinking: he's not cheating because you're not beautiful and he's not cheating because the other woman is more beautiful than you are. He's cheating because he is an adulterer and that's what adulterers do. You can place the least handsome adulterer with the most beautiful and faithful woman, and he'd still cheat on her because he is an adulterer. It has nothing to do with how we are on the outside. The best response you can give an adulterer is no response at all. You simply need to hold a

Effective Warfare Tactics

conversation with the LORD and let HIM do all of the talking.

12. You can't sex a crooked man straight. Another common response to adultery is sex. Many wives will attempt to compete with their husbands' mistresses by over-sexing their husbands. That's because the average wife thinks that she can drain her husband of all of his energy so he won't have any strength to have sex with his mistress. Then again, she may believe she can outperform the mistress. Please know that a man does not cheat because the sex at home isn't good. He cheats because he is an adulterer...period. At the same time, over-sexing a husband will only temporarily take his strength away. His body will recuperate rather quickly, and within hours (sometimes minutes), he will likely be able to perform again.

13. Never underestimate the power of silence. When you're in pain, your mind will swell with ideas and words you think you should

Effective Warfare Tactics

try on your husband. You keep trying to reason with him and get him to understand that he's hurting you, his mistress is not worth him losing his marriage, you're becoming fed up with his philandering ways, and the list goes on and on. Some women even resort to threatening to harm the mistress, and this only works in the mistress's favor. If you've told your husband you want him to be faithful, his infidelities are hurting you, and if you've made it clear to your husband that you won't stick around if he continues to cheat, you've said enough. After you have spoken with the head of your home and he refuses to honor you, the correct thing to do is go to his head (JESUS) and cast that burden upon HIM. Constantly yelling and investigating your husband won't help the situation at all. It'll only further agitate it. Every time new evidence comes to light, show it to your husband to let him know you're aware of what he's doing, and then,

Effective Warfare Tactics

keep silent. Silence scares a man who's accustomed to an argumentative woman because a talkative woman unwittingly tells her husband every piece of evidence she has. In other words, she basically tells him where he's slipping up and what he needs to do a better job at hiding. A silent woman, on the other hand, is a mystery to her husband, and for this reason, she will get her husband's attention and cause him to try and figure out what she knows. This puts pressure on him to make a decision in relation to his adulterous affair because he's not sure how much his wife knows, how much time he has left to play his games, or what she'll do next. Please note that once you start being silent, your husband will likely try to infuriate, hurt, or offend you because he wants you to open your mouth and tell him what's in your heart. Don't give in to this. Instead, do something nice for him to further confuse that devil in him; for example, bake him a

batch of cookies and tell him you love him.
14. Praise GOD whenever you can. The devil hates praise with a passion and he can't stand in the midst of true praise. Don't focus on your situation, focus on your GOD, and just praise HIM for who HE is. Your praise will confuse the enemy. Your praise will scare the enemy. Your praise will usher you into the very presence of GOD if it is pure, and the enemy will run every time he sees you approaching the Throne of GOD in praise.
15. Worship the LORD in the beauty of holiness. First and foremost, you're probably wondering what the difference is between praise and worship. Praise is a joy-filled celebration of GOD. It is to sing, dance, or shout for GOD. Worship, on the other hand, is more reverential. It is to humble yourself before GOD. Praise honors what GOD has done, but worship honors GOD for who HE is. In worship, you have to put yourself away and just

> surrender your all to HIM. Worship is not selfish, nor is it about what GOD has done or can do for you, worship is about who HE is...period. This means we are to approach GOD and worship HIM without holding anything back and without throwing our needs and desires at HIM. We simply honor and acknowledge who HE is.

Of course, there are other things you can do to effectively fight the enemy, but you have to remember that none of these things will guarantee your marriage will last. Truthfully, if your husband decides he loves his sin more than he loves you or the LORD, he will get up and flee from you once you submit yourself wholly to GOD. This isn't a bad thing, however. The thing is, he was going to leave anyway, or his plans for you may have been darker, therefore, when a man leaves his HOLY SPIRIT filled wife, it's likely because the devil in him is fleeing from the GOD in her. Although losing a spouse can be painful, it's not the end of the world. You have to think about it this way:

Effective Warfare Tactics

would you rather stay with the spouse and have him hurt you for the rest of his (or your) life, or would you rather him leave and you endure the temporary pain associated with losing a spouse?

If the spouse decides to go, please know that your heart will heal and you will live to love another day, and maybe next time, GOD will bless you with someone who loves you back.

If your husband decides to submit himself to GOD, on the other hand, you will have saved his life and won his soul over for the Kingdom of Heaven. Don't spend your time trying to figure out what's going to happen next and which way your marriage is going to go. Just live, stay in GOD'S will, and wait to see the glory of GOD and the manifestation of HIS will for your marriage. If what you want for you doesn't match what HE wants for you, you'll only delay your arrival to the place HE'S prepared for you. That's why the better prayer is: *GOD, let your will be done in my life. Not my will, but Your will.*

Effective Warfare Tactics

Surrendering wholly to GOD shows HIM you trust HIM, and a believer who trusts in the LORD is a believer who's rightly positioned to receive the blessings of GOD because that believer is standing behind HIM and letting HIM go before self.

GOD knows your pain and HE knows how much you can bear, even when you think you've reached your limits. The correct way to handle an adulterous husband is to simply hand him over to GOD and let GOD correct him. From there, GOD will give him a choice: repent and continue living in the favor he's been enjoying because of you, or leave. If he chooses to leave, he's not just walking away from you, he's walking away from his favor. Either way, you have to forgive him for what he's done, and understand this: if you're anointed and blessed of GOD, your anointing and your blessings will follow you everywhere you go. The favor of GOD will continue to live in you, and the man of GOD who finds you will obtain favor from the LORD because he's chosen to honor you. If

Effective Warfare Tactics

your husband repents and the two of you stay together, don't rub his nose in his past. Instead, allow what you've been through to draw the both of you closer to GOD, and when the two of you come to HIM together, HE will draw you closer to one another.

www.ingramcontent.com/pod-product-compliance
Lightning Source LLC
Chambersburg PA
CBHW071648090426
42738CB00009B/1459